The Nature of Ethics

Defining Ethics, Good & Evil

By

Christopher Angle

2nd Edition
Copyright © 2024 by Christopher Angle
All rights reserved

ISBN: 979-8-9877707-4-0
Library of Congress Catalogue Number 97-92852
RITE Report Inc.
100 Research Dr., Unit 16
Stamford, CT 06906
Tel. 203/253-2008
email: detmar-haskell@rite.report
Printed in the USA

Other Detmar & Haskell Dialogues in Chronological Order by Chris Angle

- *The Nature of Aesthetics*
- *Truth & The Nature of Decisions*
- *The Philosophical Equations of Economics*
- *The Nature of the Political Left & Right*

Table of Contents

The material herein will bear the influence of a professor of the University of Michigan — Frank B. Livingstone.

Prologue

Detmar and Haskell were first encountered in *The Nature of Aesthetics*. There, it was learned, Detmar is a botany professor at the University of Michigan and one of his hobbies is philosophy. He enjoys and actually encourages dialogues with students who pursue inquiry into the nature of things. Haskell is one of the students who visit Detmar, but more significantly, he is the one who most enjoys the sessions and has been known to spend considerable time with the professor.

It is an early weekday afternoon and Haskell through with his classes for the day drops by to see Detmar in his office. He knocks, opens Detmar's office door, sticks his head in, and the following transpires.

Chapter 1

The Definition of Ethics

Haskell: Good afternoon, Professor!

Detmar: Good afternoon, Haskell! Come on in. I haven't seen you in a while.

H: Yes, it's been awhile. I hope everything has been well with you, Professor.

D: Yes, very well, thank you. And I trust the same with you.

H: Oh, yes. Everything is fine, and I will enter the graduate school in philosophy next semester.

D: Congratulations. I know that was your plan. I am glad that it is being realized.

H: I would like to thank you for the time you have spent with me, and I would like to emphasize that your thinking has influenced me profoundly. As you know, I have sometimes, when the opportunity presented itself, used the subject matter of our discussions in my curriculum, and have published some of my notes from our discourse on aesthetics.

D: I hope those were well received by your professors.

H: Oh, yes. Very much so.

D: Good.

H: Professor, I wondered if you have some time this afternoon.

D: Oh, what's up?

H: Well. Some questions have come to mind that I would like to pose to you.

D: OK. What's on your mind?

H: Before I go directly into the subject, I would like to explain first that this matter is not school-related nor is it a subject of any of my classes. It is a concern that has just developed over the last year or so. I have been trying to resolve it in my mind, but I have not been able to come to any conclusion. In fact, I have made almost no headway in solving the problem, and as it is constantly on my mind and has become an important personal issue for me, with your permission I would like to bring it to your attention.

D: You know I am always keenly interested in the subjects you bring to our conversations.

H: Thank you. What I would like to discuss is the question of how one should lead one's own life, and how someone can talk about how someone else should live his life.

D: I am not quite sure what you mean. Can you elaborate a bit?

H: Throughout my life, I have heard people say to me or to other people that they should not do this with their life or should do that with their life, or that they are wasting away their life doing this or that. It is endless. Everybody has an opinion as to how somebody else should live his life. I suppose the most ready example would be the remembrances of my father telling me I should study harder, that I should go out for basketball as opposed to wrestling, that I should eat my entire dinner not neglecting the vegetables, that I should mow the lawn, or open the car door for my mother. The list is endless. But broadening the scope, although my father advised, ordered, and recommended that I do certain things, people everywhere are expressing opinions on how other people should do things and what they should do.

D: But this type of advise, orders, or recommendations from your father do not seem to be as weighty as your question of how one should live.

H: These are just examples of one person telling another person what he should do, but collectively they would seem to me to add up to how one should live. To further the examples, father would recommend or at times argue about more important problems concerning myself. He has often strongly recommended that I should go to law school as opposed to entering a post graduate curriculum of philosophy. Sometimes he has even hinted that he would not provide any funding for anything but law. He desires that I follow the same type of education that he received.

D: I assume that he went to law school?

H: Yes, he did. But what I am having trouble with is this: what is it that requires my father to recommend me to do one thing over another, or for anyone to believe that another person ought to do one thing over another thing? People have beliefs that certain actions are better than other actions and it is judgmental. What is it that makes up the essence of this judgment? For example, let's say that one person sleeps a lot, does not need to work much, hangs around home most of the day, does nothing constructive and, basically, lives a sloth-like existence. Another person goes to his employment, comes home, works around the house, has a family, and is continually busy with things, and everyone who views this person's life would say that he is industrious and probably does not have many recommendations for his life.

D: OK.

H: Who is to say that the second person's life is any better than the first person's? They both are human. They both live their lives freely; they both do not hurt anybody or impose themselves unlawfully on anybody else. Is there anything to say that inherently person number one is any less of a man than person number two? Is there anything that could lead us to a judgment of whether one life is better than another or whether one person should change his life and do something else? Is there a standard of judgment in life that will enable one person to judge or recommend another to do just as my father asserts that I should do one thing over another? Is there anything that we can look at and say - "Oh, person number one is a sloth; that is wrong; he must change" - but person number two is OK, he does not need to change?

D: I see.

H:　　Furthermore, this line of questioning should be extrapolated further to understand how is it we solve any problem of what is good and what is bad, which is right and which is wrong.　How can anybody say to anybody else that one person is wrong and another right, one fellow doing good and another is doing wrong, that this man is righteous and another is unrighteous?　I suppose I am inquiring into the essence of good and evil, right and wrong, moral and immoral, ethical and unethical.

D:　　An interesting set of questions, and it is something that a man should try to put in order in his life, and I might add that philosophers throughout history having been trying to sort out.

H:　　Yes, I believe that I am inquiring into the nature of judgment, or in other words I am looking for a system of ethics.

D:　　I see.

H:　　But even here I have a problem.　I just now said that I am seeking a system of ethics.

D:　　Yes.

H:　　It seems to me that I have a secondary problem besides that of constructing a system of ethics.　I am wondering how anyone even armed with a system of ethical judgment can believe that his way of ethical judgment is better or more comprehensive than another's, and hence, how could he say that his judgment is better than another's?

D: I am beginning to see your problem.

H: It seems to me without that high moral ground, if you will, and that belief that one's own set of moral rules is the best that one could conclude that there is no right and wrong and good and bad and so on. Because if there is no one set of ethical rules that govern supremely over all others, then there will be no saying that one person is righteous and another unrighteous, that one is good and another bad or evil. Even more importantly one cannot even say that someone is better or more virtuous than another.

D: Well, that will be an interesting subject with which to involve ourselves.

H: This problem of capacity of judgment and to know that which is ethical has been on my mind. It is just like coming out of the movies and arguing with my girl friend whether the movie was any good. Who says my judgment of a movie's content is any more correct than another's? It seems to me the same thing: how do we judge anything?

D: In making a judgment one must pick a standard that one adheres to intellectually, and when a problem comes up that is relevant, one will use the standard to make a decision and resolve the problem.

H: Like we did in our discussion of art: we defined it, satisfied ourselves that we can apply it to art and that the definition, or standard, is complete and consistent for all art.

D: Yes. So in art, we can refer to our standard to make judgment concerning literature, artistic painting, sculpture, poetry et cetera. And the same is true for other disciplines. Problems of physics are solved using the principles discovered by Newton. And now more recently by Einstein, Planck, and others. Each discipline has a standard, even for day-to-day life. Many people in making rules for their life take the Bible as their standard. When deciding how to act in society, they have the ten commandments, the proverbs, the stories of the Old Testament, and the teachings of Jesus in the New Testament to guide them.

H: Yes, but even with the Bible, there are other religions that put forth their own mantra and purport their own particular way of life. An example of this is the Muslim religion whose followers adhere to the teachings of the Koran. Although there are many similarities between the two religions, there are some differences that set them apart and would induce different behavior and solutions to problems that are encountered in day-to-day living. Hence, I am wondering which does a person select, and is a selection of one religion and its set of beliefs and teachings better than another. How does one know which standard to choose and employ to structure one's life in society?

D: One will pick his standard or an evident assumption from which to start from his best available choices or come up with one through one's own thought processes. For example, for a long time, we took Newton's laws of physics and his mathematics to explain much of the universe and how it worked. Now we know that his calculations were approximate and not absolutely precise. But they worked to explain events as we perceived them. As our perception increased in its power to perceive the minute, we found that it was not quite right. Luckily, before we began perceiving that Newton's laws were not perfect, Einstein, Planck, et al came along and saved the day with their equations predicting this, furthering our knowledge of the universe.

H: And physicists are still looking for other equations that will explain further the universe as I know they are looking for something I have heard called the "unifying theory."

D: Yes, but the point is that for a long time, and even today, the explanations work as far as they go. They are not wrong, just not as precise as other explanations. Hence, since they answer questions as completely as they do, they are something that is useful, correct, and reasonable. Without the Newtonian stepping stone, further insights and developments in physics that answer further questions would not have come about.

H: Yes.

D: We must find our starting point and develop it to our satisfaction that it is complete and consistent with all our experiences. Just because our initial inquiries into a problem lead us to preliminary answers that are reasonable but we find out later that the answers are not all-inclusive or precise enough to cover all instances in the universe, it does not make the initial answers to the initial inquiries incorrect. The initial answer, as long as it was consistent with all of our experiences and reasonable, would be correct in its initial use. The second and later set of questions challenging the initial questions and answers have a second layer of experiences that could not have been understood without the initial answers that enable the inquirer to further his knowledge and look for a second layer of answers that explain consistently the initial questions and the second tier. Hence, the first set of inquiries were not wrong, they were just not complete.

H: OK. I understand. But these are things of science. What about my question concerning religion? That is, which set of religious beliefs do we start with? This does not seem to me to be easily decided.

D: You are right, it isn't. But the same method is employed. You take your experiences in life and apply them to a set of religious precepts. People generally prefer those of the culture in which they were raised, especially in matters concerning the worship of God. However several of the major religions address the problems of how to live and set down precepts by which people of that faith should abide. And when all these precepts from all the religions come within the realm of ethics and how one should live, act, and behave in society, the basis of good and bad in behavior is dictated by survivability.

H: You mean to say that ethics is how to behave in society?

D: Yes. And its basis is the degree to which behavior lends itself to survival. That is, the more behavior in general is oriented toward survival, the more the behavior becomes ethical.

H: What? I am afraid I do not understand. How can this be? Let's go back over my initial barrage of questions and please explain how survival helps answer any of these.

D: Fine.

H: First, I can agree that ethics is the study of how one should act in the society of others, but if I understand you correctly, you say that the root of ethics by which we may understand how to act, that is the nature of ethics, is survival. You purport that the basis of any system of ethics is in survival.

D: Yes.

H: Well, how can we use this standard for ethics which you purport to be survival to understand who leads a better life: the sloth-like fellow who sleeps, eats, and does very little or the energetic hard-working fellow?

D: Using the measure of survival, we can clearly say that the hard-working fellow is more in line with good ethical behavior because he is advancing his life, preparing to advance his career and future, and probably saving money in case a rainy day comes along.

H: You mean to say that because our fellow is industrious, while another is not, the diligent fellow is behaving more ethically only because his industrious character relates closely to survivability.

D: Yes.

H: And that this concept of survival is how we judge all behavior and whether one aspect of behavior is better than another and how one is more ethically better than another.

D: Yes.

H: I am not sure what to say at this point except to ask if you could iterate the definition of ethics and then elaborate a bit on it to get us moving.

D: Certainly, ethics is the judgment of proper behavior, it is the critique of good and bad in behavior, and the essence of the good and bad in behavior is respect. That is, the more respectful an action, the more it is ethical. Ethics is the degree of respect in behavior.

H: That's it? What you have just said is that ethics is based on respect.

D: Yes. That is correct.

H: But just a minute ago you said that it is based on survival.

D: Yes. All behavior is rooted in survival. All life's first purpose is to survive; that is, the DNA of the cell operates to make itself survive at least long enough to reproduce itself for continued survival. First, survival of itself, then extended survival by reproduction.

H: Yes, I agree. But what does this have to do with respect and ethics which you say are the same? You seem to equate respect with survival.

D: All behavior of the cell or congregations of cells can be found ultimately in its want and need for survival. But the world has seen an evolution of groups of cells that have emanated from a mother cell into an organism. The organisms have become complex, and social behavior evolved whereby some of the organisms band together sociably in order to further insure their complex survival. Man, of course, is one of these organisms that requires an element of social compatibility and the ability to congregate amicably to insure the survival of the species.

H: Yes, biology and anthropology books are full of explanations of this evolution of man and how it necessarily required a component of sociability and that this was needed when man's predecessor's environment changed and they found themselves gradually pushed onto the plains of Africa. A division of labor and the ability to cooperate between themselves evolved, and this behavioral component of cooperation is integral to their ability to survive.

D: The vehicle by which man is able to cooperate with other human beings which insures his group's survival is respect. It is from this feeling of respect for the other person in one's society that ethics is produced. The study of ethics is the amount and degree and kind of respect one person gives others in his society.

H: Therefore, I take it that the more one respects his fellow man, the more he is ethical.

D: Yes.

H: Then just because I am respectful to my parents means that I am an ethical person at least in regards to my parents.

D: Yes, when you act ethically to your parents, each ethical action, in fact, all your behavior, if it is ethical, is a respectful action. And conversely, if it is a respectful action, then it is ethical.

H: Are there no ethical actions that do not contain respect; that is, is it absolutely necessary that all ethical actions have respect?

D: Yes. It is the necessary ingredient by which the ethical arises. After all, the ethical is that behavior that is the proper way to act, and the proper way is that which is based on survival. Hence, any action is judged on whether it promotes the survival of life and concretely, the life-controlling DNA. This is exemplified by the survival of the life and specifically the DNA molecules of the organism long enough to reproduce to insure the continuance of the gene.

H: Have you ever seen two dogs that are given their meals, and when one finishes before the other, the faster one tries to take the food of the slow one? If two men are wolfing down their dinners and one finishes his dinner faster than the other and then attacks the second man to obtain his food, he is surely not acting ethically but he is providing himself with food and hence is insuring himself his own survival. By his action of obtaining more food, he is making certain that he will have enough food until the next time he is hungry.

D: Yes, I said that ethics is based on survival, but the survival of mankind is also dependent on respect. Hence, the action is unethical because there was no respect when the one man attacked the other for the food. The action by itself helps the one man survive on a short-term basis because one must eat to survive, but in consideration of the long term, the production of food requires actions of respect.

H: In what way?

D: All respect induces cooperation and that is the essence of respect. The need for cooperation arose to enable man to become societal. The vehicle by which cooperation is effected is the condition of respect.

H: Well, you say that cooperation is the end for which respect appeared. But what is it that makes up respect by which cooperation appears?

D: That would be consideration. When you consider another person when you do an action, you have the beginning of respect.

H: You mean to consider it in a good way. I take it that we must add that one considers the needs and presence of others around you and acts with one's own needs in mind yet acts in accordance and harmony with the others around you.

D: Precisely.

H: Then, to reiterate, consideration of others in one's actions makes up respect, and respect is the key to cooperation which is necessary for the survival of mankind.

D: And ethics is the behavior that has respect inherent in it. Any action that a person takes, if it includes respect, necessarily is ethical in some way. If one's actions have respect, then one's behavior is ethical.

H: And how is it again that all that is related to ethics has its basis in survival?

D: There are two dimensions to surviving: the first dimension is the individual acquiring his needs from that which is around him, that is, his environment; the second dimension is cooperating with others in the same predicament to mutually, together through cooperation, obtain the things in life that one desires. This cooperation is effected by the appearance of respect. Respect is the vehicle that humans use to promote cooperation between themselves.

H: So in order to cooperate you need respect?

D: Yes

H: Surely not. There are animals that cooperate together, and when they do, can you call it respect?

D: Cooperation, even among animals, has the rudiments of respect because respect is consideration of others in one's behavior which enables cooperation. So if one ant in passing another ant, stops to identify itself or do whatever ants do when they pass each other, the ants are being considerate of each other and are communicating cooperation, and this is the basis of respect. If, hypothetically, the female of some species, whatever it is, allows its young or the male mate to eat its catch before she does, this is out of respect. The reason for her cooperation may be varied. She may let her mate eat because of his powerful size, and if he does not eat first, he may do something awful. She is respecting his power. She may let her young ones eat because she wants to insure their survival, and her cooperation with letting them eat is a sign of respecting their lives and upbringing and their surviving her.

H: I see. And this cooperation is needed to sustain life. But how is respect manifested? This one animal deferring to the power of another is nothing else but submission. Might here is making right. Is this ethical that the powerful be over the weak whether the situation is present in the animal kingdom or in mankind?

D: Respect comes from the language of submission which is a kind of consideration, and hence, submissive forms of communication demonstrate respect, and inwardly, it is the consideration of others as one does something that involves another. It does not matter what are the peculiar ways that a group of animals or humans cooperate, whether it is by the powerful gaining preference by virtue of their strength, by intelligence obtaining domination over the less intelligent, or the athletically adroit gaining physical prominence. What matters is that there is some consistent, cooperative manner of behavior that enables the group or a society of individuals to survive, and the more successful it is in proliferating and becoming ecologically successful, the more the particular mannerisms of the group manifest themselves as the best way for the society, and this behavior becomes an ethic in the population's behavior.

H: I think I see. A troop of baboons would pivot on the strength of the dominant male and his behavior demands cooperation through his individual power.   When he demonstrates his strength, others will show a submissive sign indicating compliance and nonaggression.

D: Yes, this nonaggression is a sign of respect of the dominate male's strength.   Yet the group stays together because it needs to in order to survive individually and in total. An individual baboon would not last long on the plains of Africa.   The individual does not muster as much self-defense as the group can to fend off predators.   When the baboon troop is threatened by a predator, the male baboons rally together, cooperating together to face the outside threat in force. These males are able to do this by dropping their aggression toward each other thereby enabling them to cooperate to face an enemy together.

H: And when they drop this aggression toward each other, whether it is animal or man, they can cooperate together, and when there is cooperation, there is respect.

D: Yes, in the case of the baboons facing an outside aggressor, the males know that in order for them as individuals and as a group to survive they must drop their individual aggressions, consider the good of the others around them, and band together with the others to produce a safe haven for their little society by warding off the outside threat.

H: So even at this rudimentary level of behavior, there can be respect for others.

D: Yes, respect is resultant from the need to cooperate and the behavioral vehicle that respect employs is submission.

H: I thought you said that the basis of respect was consideration. What is the difference between submission and consideration?

D: Consideration is to think of another in forming one's actions and submission is one form of this.

H: Then in a complicated society such as man's, respect becomes, of course, exponentially more important as more and more cooperation is needed. It would be seen that man's societal culture depends on cooperation.

D: You bet. Societal culture began with the appearance of consideration of others in behavior. Culture is the interaction with one's surroundings physically and socially, and the makeup of social culture is the degree of consideration that people have for one another. The extent to which we consider persons in our society dictates how well-developed our behavior culture is.

H: Then, as I understand it, there is a connection between the degree of respect and the extent of our culture.

D: In our interactions with others in our society it is the extent to which we consider others that determines how well-developed our culture is and the outward behavioral manifestation (such as hand shakes, salutes, polite language) of this consideration is respect. That is, the more respect that we have, the more culture we have.   Behavioral culture depends on respect for others as well as respect for oneself. And anything that is culture will be within the production of the physical things of society or within the behavior of consideration and respect.

H: So there are two sides to culture.   The first part of culture is the physical side.

D: Yes.   If one interacts with his surroundings by inventing a hammer, nails, and a saw and builds a home with these tools, he is developing a physical culture for himself. If this home is just a one-room hut, then an anthropologist would observe that this man's physical culture is rudimentary. If he invents elaborate tools and builds himself a complicated home with many bedrooms, plumbing, lights, and instruments with which to cook, an anthropologist would observe that this man has a developed physical culture.

H: And the second part of culture is the societal culture which began with the appearance of consideration for others in behavior.

D: Yes. In a primitive culture when the first hominid long ago came out of its general selfishness and increased its actions of harmony, cooperation, or deference to another, you had the first elements of the non-physical human culture. As the greater the cooperation between individuals evolved, more respect was needed, and therefore, social culture appeared. The evolutionary adaptative purpose of respect which evolved from the language of submission (consideration) is to reduce aggression and tension between individuals promoting the ability to cooperate. This cooperation is needed to produce things necessary to construct a standard of living. Hence, this consideration of others, or respect, is commensurate with production. That is, the more an individual produces, the more he is respected by others.

H: That is quite a statement. Are you serious?

D: Certainly.

H: Well, I suppose in the case of the baboon or other lower animal societies production means the rudimentary efforts of gathering food and staying alive. However, in advanced civilization, man's production goes beyond just getting the day's food. Hence, the production takes on a greater significance.

D: Yes. Production is the gage that we use in the amount of respect we give another. We respect the mailman for the mail that he delivers, we respect the factory worker for his day's labor. We esteem the president of a large company to a further extent because of the large quantities of items of which he is coordinating the production that people seek to buy and use in their lives. Moreover, we can respect a fellow man whom we know nothing about as a fellow man. We can do this because we know that people produce something in order to live, get paid, and live a normal life as a citizens somewhere. To that extent, we accord that certain amount of respect when in daily contact with other human beings. On the other hand, an indigent who does not have a job, a place to live, produces nothing, and has no purpose in society will not command much respect. Conversely, the person who gives employment to many and uses many means to produce much will command great respect from all whom he meets on a business level.

H: Then would we respect a businessman the most in a society that produces many goods and services?

D: We would respect him considerably but not necessarily the most. But in every case, respect comes from production of something, and it does not have to be physical things or actual goods by a manufacturer that produces a profit. It can be a professor who produces teachings that students gather around to
assimilate. It can be a mother who produces nourishment and care for a young one. The mother who gestates, bears a baby, and takes care of it is producing a product and service most valued by her husband and family and herself; and where there is production by oneself and valued by oneself there is self-respect. The mother and the professor are respected for their non-material service-oriented products just as is the industrialist. Respect is based on production of something that is valued by another or others.

H: You just mentioned self-respect?

D: Self-respect is also based on production. Loss of self-respect is when we do not achieve a goal in producing something that we feel that we should have produced. We know our own capacity to produce and our self-respect is the measure of how well we meet our own particular goals of this production.

H: I see.

D: We now can understand that a decline in a behavioral culture is necessarily tied to a decline in respect because respect is a necessary component of culture and the essence of respect is consideration of others when making one's decisions how to act. Its purpose is to promote cooperation which facilitates the production of goods and services which furthers the survival of mankind.

H: Then, as I understand it, production is the end result to which culture and its components of tools, goods, services, respect, and consideration strive. The impetus for the existence of production comes from the basic instinct to survive and from the self-interest of the desire to live better.

D: Yes. We must produce to survive. At the very least humans had to hunt and gather food, the very most basic type of production. Fortunately, in Homo Sapiens there evolved more intelligence, and the self-interest to exist took a step further by looking for opportunities to improve one's existence by seeking ways to further production ultimately for consumption. Not only do we look to exist as does every other species on earth, but we are imbued with a desire and ability to improve our lot, and hence, comes our desire to improve our production for further consumption. The more production and consumption there is per capita, the farther we are from bare existence which helps to insure our survival. We see that self-interest to live better initiates the desire for production of goods and services. However, in order to facilitate group effort in production, consideration is needed. Cooperation is made possible by the consideration of others which is respect which constitutes social culture, which is one aspect of culture in general.

H: So, if we were to outline this thought process, we could express it as, first, self-interest; then this would lead to the consideration of others which is made possible by the use of respect which is the essence of ethics which is the appropriate dispensation of respect which allows for cooperation to produce things and services which becomes a society's physical and behavioral cultures.

D: Excellent!

H: I think I have been able to follow our conversation, but I doubt if I have an integral, comprehensive understanding of ethics yet. Could we go over it again in a summary fashion?

D: Surely. We established that ethics is the study of good and bad in social behavior and the word "social" is necessary here because where there is only the individual alone and there is no society for him with which to interact, ethics does not exist for that individual.

H: Because he is alone?

D: Right. Without society, there is no ethics. There is no right or wrong. The only question that exists for a lone being is what is good or bad in the ability to survive as an individual. As he does not have to think of others in what he does to survive, the concern of that which is ethical cannot enter his mind and is irrelevant to his situation.

H: Why?

D: Because he must only do what it takes to benefit his survival. No other survival is in question. His self-interest dictates that he will do what is good for his own survival and since there is not the second dimension of others around him, he does not have to consider others, and therefore his actions can only be one dimensional in whether the action is good or not. He only thinks of himself and therefore that which is ethical behavior is not an issue.

H: I see. But you said previously that ethics is that behavior that is based on survival. You say that this lone man's actions are not within the realm of ethics because he is alone, not that he has questions that relate to survival. But I believe he has questions of survival, therefore it seems according to what you have said that he has questions of ethics.

D: Yes, I said that, but I also mentioned that man's survival cannot depend on himself alone, at least not for long. If a man is one of those mountain men that we used to read about back in the 19th century who would disappear into the wilderness for a long while, their survival depended only on themselves and they were not with, nor wanted to be with, other people. With the lone mountain man we consider the short-term survival of one man, and seeing that he is not in contact with others he has no problems with ethics. But if he comes into contact with others and interacts with them, then ethics comes into his life because he is cooperating at least to some small degree with these people. As one cooperates with another, he is benefiting from others as he is in concert with others as they go about surviving. And as mankind in order to survive must be social, ethics is essential. If the world were made up of mountain men only, the world would soon lose its population altogether and the human species would not survive. As mankind can only survive in groups together in society, ethics necessarily exists through man's need to cooperate with each other and each action of behavior that we would consider good or bad, ethical or unethical, is determined by how it relates to the survival of mankind.

H: I see so far that the existence of ethics requires society and the standard by which we can understand ethics is that behavior which is given to the survival of society.

D: Yes. If an action by someone lends itself to the good of himself and others, it is an ethical action, and the more good the action does, the more ethical it is.

H: And this good action is ethical because a good action helps people survive.

D: Correct.

H: You also mentioned that ethical action is dependent on respect and cooperation. Could you explain that again?

D: All right.   God initiated in life a will to live and continue to live. The basic mechanical component of living things is DNA.   The DNA, the holder of life's information, in order to help itself live, wraps itself in a cell to protect itself from the environment.   Its next project is to reproduce to make more of itself furthering its chances of survival. DNA further finds out that it is more efficacious in a hostile environment to reproduce a bunch of cells and then band together in association with these cells all coming from a mother cell to form an organism. This furthers its ability to survive.

H: Yes, this scenario is described in great detail in texts devoted to evolution.

D: Right. One set of organisms evolved mechanisms to provide its food from sunlight, minerals, and water and a second set of organisms made a living by devouring other DNA-containing cells.

H: The plant and animal kingdoms.

D: Correct. The organisms of the animal kingdom became hostile to each other because it became a maze of all these different organisms eating other organisms.

H: The food chain develops.

D: And in order to survive, many organisms, as the individual cells realized earlier, learned to band together further facilitating the survival of its DNA.

H: Group organization appears and so does cooperation.

D: Yes. Once again, when the DNA of the cells realized that cooperation led to a further increased rate of survival and went ahead to assemble the organism, to coordinate a cellular cooperative association, cells began to specialize.

H: The division of labor.

D: One type of cell that was necessary was one that could coordinate information between the cells so that they could act in concert in attaining their means to survival.

H: Nerve cells and then ultimately the brain.

D: Hence, the information processing cells and the other means by which the cells communicate are the glue that helps the organism's cells act in unison and cooperate toward the goal of surviving in the environment.

H: OK

D: In the DNA's tertiary step of insuring its survival it causes, directly or indirectly, the organisms to act in concert together obtaining its means of subsistence and defending itself from the other DNA eaters. And in order to act in concert, cooperative behavior must evolve to enable an association of like organisms to act together performing the analogous function as the nerve and brain cells and the other communicative means do for the individual organism.

H: So, the ability of organisms to cooperate is analogous to the communicative means of the body's collective cells in a single organism.

D: Yes. Just as in a single organism, the brain does most of the coordination between the organs in the body, the ability to cooperate coordinates the individual organisms. And this ability to cooperate is through respect, and respect is the consideration of the other individual. This development of consideration in the organism determines how well the organisms can cooperate with each other. Furthermore, the development of consideration is the essence of culture.

H: How is that again? Consideration provides culture?

D: To review what we discussed before, the way our consideration of the others around us, which is respect, determines our social culture, and when this consideration is used for cooperation in the group production of physical things that help us survive, then we see the development of physical culture.

H: I see.

D: And when organisms congregate, all behavior that is outside the consideration of the others in the group in its group effort to further its survival is unethical, and all behavior that has this consideration of others inherent in the actions - respectful behavior - is ethical behavior.

H: Thank you, Detmar. I believe I am now grasping the essence of ethics. To further this inquiry I would like to ask about some related concepts that I suspect fall under the study of ethics.

D: Such as?

H: Well, I would like to ask you what is justice.

D: Good problem.

Chapter 2

Justice, Contracts, Rights, Value, The Good, Virtue

H.How is justice of ethics? I believe that Aristotle said that it has to do with giving a man what is due to him.

D: Yes. Justice is that which should be due a person according to the various contracts that a person has entered into. And those understandings that reside within a contract are rights and obligations.

H: Justice is the upholding of contracts, and rights and obligations are the contractual understandings?

D: Yes. And should the process of contract sanctity go away, the rectification of the aberration is also within the process of justice.

H: You are referring to the breaking of a law, or a social contract as Locke might have said and the rectification of this by appropriate penalty or punishment (which of course sometimes is forgiven) - this setting things straight - is part of the process of the upholding of contracts.

D: Yes.

H: And I suppose that all justice is of the realm of ethics?

D: Yes.   Ethics is the judgment of good and bad in behavior and justice is the adherence to the sanctity of contract which is good and is ethical; and this, as you pointed out about Aristotle, is giving a man his due according to the various contracts he has entered into. Justice is of ethics. All justice is within the realm of ethics as justice is the adherence to contracts and the sanctity of contracts is considered good for society.

H: So, that social behavior that is ultimately oriented toward survival which will have that behavior that has consideration in it is of the ethical and the adherence to this standard of behavior is justice.   Any aberration from this standard is unjust.

D: Yes. You are correct. And the process of rectification of the contractually unethical to the contractually ethical is the process of justice. The province of justice does not concern itself with all of ethics. Justice is only concerned with ethical behavior that involves contracts - social, written, unwritten, implied or otherwise.

H: How is that?

D: If I met an indigent on the street, I have extra money, and I give some money to him, I believe I am acting in an ethical fashion.   If somebody is injured before my eyes in some sort of an accident such as a car, skiing, or just a slip on the sidewalk and I take it upon myself to help the person, I believe   that   my action is ethical. And it is ethical because it ultimately is a survival-oriented action. It is effected by my consideration of the person before me. It is my respect for the fellow denizen of my surroundings that enables me to extend this consideration.

H: Yes, so far so good.

D: However, it is not a just or unjust act. If I walk past the needy person without donating anything to his cause, my action is not unjust nor could it be called an injustice. And conversely, if I help him, it is not necessarily a just act.

H: I see. There is no contract between you and the indigent person or between you and the injured fellow.

D: That's right. There has to be some sort of previous understanding with the party with whom I am interacting for justice to enter the picture. Justice is relevant if the actions between the people pertain to a previous understanding.

H: Well, what do you mean by a contract? You certainly do not mean only some written document between two parties. I suppose you are using this sense of contract in its largest most all-inclusive sense.

D: Absolutely. As you know, there are all sorts of contracts starting from the most important such as a covenant with God, as the one Abraham had, to a social contract between a people and their government as discussed by Locke, a civil law written by a representative government for its people, to a written agreement between two business parties, or just a verbal understanding between two acquaintances.

H: Yes. These are all examples of what could be called a contract. But I wondered if we could actually define the meaning of a contract. I suppose we could check that term in the dictionary.

D: A contract or agreement is a mutual realization that two or more entities must or should mutually provide and receive considerations; or that is, it is when considerations are expected to be mutually given and received.

H: I need further clarification.

D: When two or more parties interact, it is either for the purpose of friendship (intentionally social), production (business) or it is a chance social event (unintentionally social).   In every case, there are at least some societal contracts in place.

H: You mean a social contract between people of society that indicates to each other in essence that we will band together and cooperate because to do so helps promote our survival individually and as a group.

D: Right. Of course, initially, this is not written down and probably not even spoken, but people know it and understand it.   Even animals have some degree of cooperation between themselves in order to promote their survival as we discussed already.

H: Yes, I agree but does the existence of cooperation mean necessarily that a contract is in place?

D: When two people cross paths in society we expect them to be mutually civil so that they may cross paths peacefully and proceed about their purposes. We have developed social actions that communicate our nonaggressive, cooperative interactions, such as the nod, the bow, the hand shake, even the glance, and then the look away. All indicate intent or agreement to cooperate and to be non-aggressive. All are indications of respect.

H: Yes.

D: When two people come together for business which is for the purpose to exchange production, an agreement is made to exchange something of one party for something of the other party.

H: Now, could you reiterate again what is a contract, agreement, or covenant?

D: Surely. We can say that a contract, covenant, or agreement is a communication of an intent to trust for a mutual conveyance of actions or goods (i.e., the considerations) to proceed.

H: I think I understand this in a social situation. If two people come to meet on their way to somewhere on a public passageway and one person nods to the other to proceed first, and after the first proceeds, the second also proceeds unencumbered, this would be a simple social contract. It was indicated and accepted that after one person proceeded through the intersection, the other would proceed unencumbered by the first.

D: Right.

H: But how does this cover real modern-day business contracts?

D: In business, the contract would be the communication of a trust that a mutual conveyance of production will proceed.

H: You are speaking of a barter situation, but in most cases, money is used.

D: Well, we are coming very close to launching ourselves into a different discussion which might be left for another time, but let it suffice for the moment that money represents production. Without production, money cannot exist. Money is an efficiency by which production (goods and services) becomes mutually conveyed.

H: Yes, that's fine. So, going back to the definition of an agreement or contract we can say that it is an expectation of a mutual conveyance of considerations. I suppose it is no coincidence that in a bill of sale the word "consideration" is used as in "for the consideration of one dollar".

D: Yes, good point. A consideration is being equated with a dollar. In other words, we are considerate of the trading partner to the extent of one dollar for his conveyance to us of his good or service.

H: This brings us back to the essence of cooperation: that consideration of the other person is needed to cooperate with him and that consideration of the other is the essence of respect.

D: Yes. You are respecting the good or service of either person to the extent of one dollar. The extent that you respect the good or service is its value. The extent to which you respect anything is the extent to which you value that something.

H: Yes, I see that now. And justice is the consummation of a contract which is a mutual conveyance of considerations which is the respect of a good or service of another the extent of which is the magnitude of its values.

D: Yes. Justice is the reason that a contract can proceed and be consummated. Surrounding the contract there is a trust that the contract will be consummated to the reasonable expectations of both parties. In order for a contract to proceed each party is putting his trust somewhere whether it be in the other party or to a third party in whom it will be reasonable to trust in the consummation of the contract.

H: Why is there this introduction of a "third party."

D: If there is little trust in your partner, then for the contract to proceed, a third party will be sought in whom the parties can place their trust. In business, trust is known as credit. If the credit of the other party is no good, a third party is sought, such as a bank in which a party's trust (credit) can be accepted.

H: And I surmise that this is why in international agreements for conveyance of goods both parties not knowing each other or having a common government in which to place their trust will place their trust in their banks to ensure the proper conveyance. This is known in business as a bank letter of credit.

D: Yes.

H: But wait. I think we need to now define trust.

D: Trust is the probable fulfillment of a covenant or contract.

H: What was expectation?

D: The probable fulfillment of a contingency.

H: So the difference between trust and expectation is the upgrading of a contingency to a contract?

D: Correct. We are narrowing the contingency, or thing that may happen, to a specific contract that will probably happen. That is, a contract is one kind of a contingency, and hence, expecting the probable fulfillment of a covenant is the same thing as trusting in the probable fulfillment of a contract. However, when the eventuality or contingency is not of a contractual nature, then trust is impossible to be present and the situation becomes an expectation of the fulfillment of a probable event.

H: Let me ask what is the difference between trust and faith?

D: Faith is the same as trust except that the probability factor is taken out. Faith is the belief that the fulfillment of a covenant is a certainty. Faith is personal certainty in the absolute future fulfillment of a covenant or contract.

H: Just one last question in this regard.

D: Surely.

H: What would you say is poetic justice? It seems to me that it is what should have been.

D: Poetic justice is the fulfillment of an ethical situation where no contract was in place, but should or could have been in place.

H: I see. Now let me ask you about a few other related terms: good, virtue, and morality.

D: Good is directly equivalent to the ethical except it is more inclusive. The ethical is that which promotes survival in behavior, and the good is that which promotes survival. Thus, the ethical is that which is good in behavior.

H: Yes. That makes sense. But it seems to me that there are good things that do not necessarily promote survival such as the stars or the Grand Canyon, or trees. It seems to me that these things are neutral in relation to survival.

D: If you do not consider these things to be good and that they are neutral, then these things have no bearing at all on the survival of the human species. If you do not consider a tree to be good (or bad), then it is because you do not see any connection between the tree and yourself and the human species in general. However, if you consider that the tree and trees in general take in carbon dioxide and pump out oxygen which is essential for life in general and human life in particular, and that they provide wood to make habitations, then you would consider trees as good. If you do not recognize that trees provide these things, then you might not consider that trees are good.

H: You're right. When I see them in that light I feel that a tree is good. But what about something that is so unrelated to the human condition such as stars.

D: It falls under the same reasoning except that one must extrapolate further in seeing their good.

H: How so?

D: Stars are part of the universe that were born of the same energy and mechanics that the sun and earth were born. As the stars represent this creation and the very birth and evolution of the universe, they represent the goodness of creation of which the human species is a part.

H: I see. And how would you tie in the Grand Canyon to be good?

D: It is good if you consider that the geographical forces that made the Grand Canyon are the same ones that shaped your present surroundings where you presently live or where you lived before. The forces and physical laws that have made the Grand Canyon are the ones that have produced this earth which is home to you, your antecedents, and all of humankind. If you connect these considerations with the Grand Canyon, then you could or would consider the Grand Canyon inherently good. However, if you do not make this connection between human survival and the force, or forces, that created the stars or the beauty of valleys and gorges, then you would not be able to see any common good that inherently lies within these objects or their antecedents.

H: Yes, this is synchronous with what I wrote from our first conversation, *The Nature of Aesthetics.* So now, how about virtue?

D: Virtue is of the good. But it confines itself to the good that pertains to the human species - either behavior or physical characteristics. Hence, virtue is the good behavior (and we may add the good physical characteristics) that a person possesses. Morality is more limited yet. It is the good that pertains to contractual, cooperative behavior. Moral behavior is good behavior and good is that which promotes survival. Hence, morality is the cooperative, contractual behavior that promotes survival.

H: It sounds to me that morality is a sub-set of ethical behavior.

D: Yes.

H: Well, I think that concludes my inquires along these lines. I would like to ask you about something that is unjust or unethical and which is a central problem for theologians, polemicists, and apologists. What do you think evil is and what is its nature? It would be a bit too simple to think that evil would be that which is unethical, I have a feeling it should be something more. It doesn't seem enough to just describe it as unethical; it appears to be much more powerful than just that. After all, it seems to be connected to all the suffering, wrongdoing, and misery on earth. What would you say, Detmar?

D: Yes. I understand. It is a most difficult question. One that pervades Christian and other religious apologetics and is a tough philosophical conundrum.

H: Yes. It is indeed. Do you have any ideas as to its nature?

D: Let me gather my thoughts on this and let's start on it tomorrow.

H: OK, fine. I'll drop by around the same time tomorrow.

D: Fine. I look forward to it.

H: Thank you, Detmar, and I'll see you tomorrow.

D: Good day, Haskell.

Chapter 3

The Nature of Evil

It is the afternoon of the next day and the door to Detmar's office is ajar, Haskell knocks and sticks his head into the room and hails a salutation to Detmar.

H: Professor! Good afternoon.

D: Haskell, come in. Glad you could come. Today's interview I suspect will carry an interesting subject or two. I went over the problem that you brought up yesterday.

H: About the problem of evil?

D: Yes.

H: I know that Christian apologists have a difficult time with evil because it is difficult to explain away, and it is probably the atheist's strongest argument by saying that the existence of evil disproves that God is totally good which is a contradiction. Also, there is an unjust dispensation of evil; even if one is good, that person still may befall misery, mishap, or just pure evil.

D: Yes. It is a famous problem.

H: But all the arguments seem to me to be incomplete in some way. They do not seem to analyze the problem to my satisfaction.

D: I see. How do you want to pursue this topic?

H: I would like to start the way I usually do by asking for a definition of evil so that at least we know what it is and its essence. I mentioned yesterday that evil might be the unethical, but I have my doubts. It seems to me that this definition is not inclusive enough. I would think that there must be at least another ingredient to the definition than just being unethical.

D: Yes, there is. Let me provide your missing ingredient by saying that evil is the disrespect of others with an unethical objective.

H: I'm sorry Detmar, but this may take some explaining as I don't really follow you.

D: Not at all.

H: First, you indicated that the second ingredient is disrespectfor the individual.

D: Yes. Evil has two components: a disrespect of the individual and an unethical objective.   When a person machinates an objective that is unethical and abandons his respect or has no respect for the people around him when trying to realize his unethical goal, he becomes evil.

H: Really? It would seem to me to require a little more than that to become evil. After all, Hitler and Pol Pot, who in everybody's historical viewpoint that I know, were terrible villains, and it seems that they were more than just disrespectful to people - they were murderous. And of course, it is a tremendous understatement to say that their motives were unethical. Their motives were pure evil.

D: Yes, I agree.

H: In fact, it would seem to me that the answer to evil would lie in the individual's objective only, its degree of how bad his objective is and the individual's striving for it. When we take a look at Hitler or Pol Pot's objective, we recoil in horror and think how terribly bad or evil these two people were. It is not enough to say that they were unethical and their objectives were unethical. They were more than unethical.

D: True.

H: Hence, I feel that it is not enough just to say that the objective be unethical. It definitely seems that evil is more than that. It is frequently heard that somebody does something unethical as the politicians often use this term toward each other, but I would not say that they are evil.

D: Yes, I agree with you. Often somebody might be called unethical as in the political arena, but with each case, there would be lacking one of the two ingredients thereby excluding the politician from the evil category.

H: How so?
D: The unethical politician is, of course, not evil as you pointed out. But it is because his objective cannot be said to be unethical. He is fighting for some cause that he has in mind or for which his constituents have elected him.

Although others of the opposite party might not be in agreement with his objective, they would not declare his objective unethical. And not being in agreement with each other's objective would be on the rare side. Usually, politicians fight not over the objective, but the means to the objective. They all declare that education is good, that poor people should be raised somehow out of their impoverished situation, and so on.

H: So, how can he be declared unethical if his objective is declared ethical?

D: He would become unethical if he were on his way to fulfilling his objective become disrespectful. That is, if his methods to his objective were to be disrespectful to the people he is dealing with, or if he is perceived to be inconsiderate in dealing with the other politicians or not playing by the same rules that the other politicians play by, he would be considered to be unethical.

H: Yes, I suppose.

D: You also spoke about your thought that evil started at some degree of becoming unethical, that it is not enough to have both ingredients; but it must be something more; that it is not enough just to be disrespectful and unethical in order to be evil, that there must be a blatant heap of the unethical to attain the rank of evil.
H: Yes.

D: It is only that at this point you are thinking of one of the world's great examples of evil. There, the two components of evil are accentuated perfectly, and it seems that it is not enough just to say that there must be disrespect to the individuals with whom you are dealing because in Hitler's case, he was exterminating, executing, torturing, and starting wars; it is not enough to point out that his objective is unethical because he was attempting a pogrom. For him and a few others, it is clear that they were evil. But nevertheless, even though the ingredients of the definition are easily filled by these examples, we will find shortly that the definition will serve us especially when considering examples of evil that are not so clearly evil. Your objection is not that these ingredients or this definition are not satisfactory so much as it seems that the ingredients are over-satisfied, and hence there might be more to it.

H: How do you mean?

D: First, we must consider that there are degrees of evil. We mentioned examples that are close to pure intense evil. But upon examination, we will find that it will not be readily easy to satisfy both ingredients of the definition to qualify as evil.   Secondly, when someone does fulfill the two components of the definition, he will be at least to some degree evil.   The degree to which that person is evil is commensurate to the degree that person is unethical in objective and how disrespectful he is toward people of his society.

H: And so there are degrees of evil, and if you fulfill the definition, it is a matter from then on of what degree or intensity there is evil.

D: Correct.

H: But I am not satisfied with this. How do we know this definition is correct or that there are not other components of evil? The two examples of Hitler and Pol Pot, or other past political evil-doers, fit the parameters of not having an ethical objective - to reiterate the understatement - and they were disrespectful to the people around them and in their society - another understatement. It seems that when a person has these two parameters, they have just the beginnings of evil.

D: When a person has an unethical objective and disrespects the individual about him, you are correct, he has the beginnings of evil. A person in life has many objectives; it would be rare indeed to find one with all his objectives unethical or disrespectful to all that come in to contact with him. If he did, or that is, if he were disrespectful to all and all his objectives unethical, he would be thoroughly and obviously evil. When one has unethical objectives, and he is disrespectful to those who are in his way to the unethical objective, he has the characteristics of evil for that portion of his life because he has fulfilled the criteria.

H: So when a person has an immediate objective that is unethical and is inconsiderate to someone in obtaining that wrongful objective, for that portion of his life evil has entered it and we may say that he did evil for that period and after that, he is not evil.

D: Yes. Consider your own life: how many times have you had an unethical wrongful objective and tried to fulfill it? Usually to fulfill the wrongful objective, you would run across someone who will object to the goal because it is a wrongful aim and should be objected to. But you nevertheless pushed past that objection to secure, demonstrate, or finalize the objective.

H: Not many. And the only incident or two that I can think of were when I was quite young.

D: Yes. And that brings up something important. You said that it was when you were young. Your sense of the ethical was probably not complete and known to yourself. You also were more emotional and uncontrollable, and your reasoning was not complete.

H: Yes. And I still probably for the most part fit into those categories.

D: I would surmise that the evil of the great wrongdoers of history is of people who carried this incompleteness of emotional maturation and incomplete development of the ethical in their youth into adulthood. They did not develop into mature well-balanced individuals, obviously, but slid back into a situation of developing an aberration of their ethical feeling; that is, their ethical understandings were never complete in the first place, I suspect.

H: But occasionally you have heard of stories where something happens to somebody or some dreadful incident occurs in somebody's life and it changes them. For example, there are plenty of stories in literature of people being changed by their experiences of war or by encountering something drastic or even evil in their lives. Somehow a transformation takes place in their outlook on life or some particular facet of life and they begin to approach it differently or at least with a different point of view, and what was once of importance becomes less important and something new grows within and becomes an objective. Sometimes this new point of view that brings with it a new objective can be anywhere from good and nice like someone just discovering Bach or Beethoven and deciding that music is important in his life and that he must study it from now on to something terrible, such as, one's offspring or spouse is killed somehow by somebody and a parent takes to vengeance upon the perpetrator.

D: Yes, I see your point. But when the change is one of terrible moments such as vengeance, the incident of influence did not initiate a change in the manner of thinking or motivation of the individual. The individual's thought processes are unmoved by the incident. First, he had the potential to react at anytime to such stimulus. It is not a new point of view. He knew that the manslaughter of another's offspring is intrinsically and always bad, and to his mind vengeance is a natural and rightful consequence of the unfortunate mishap. In fact, he feels that his will toward vengeance may be ethical and perfectly acceptable behavior. You mentioned this example because of your perception that the law and government would handle these matters and our vengeful one has turned unethical in the incident. But you need to be aware that our vengeful one is not operating under the same principles and believes himself to be rightful and his objective to be ethical, and therefore we would be hard-pressed to understand him to be evil. We would need to unequivocally show his cause to be completely unethical.

H: Well perhaps that was an inappropriate example, but I believe that an accident can happen in a person's life that changes him and he can move to an unethical position just as my music example indicated a person can change toward the value of knowledge of music in his life.   In other words, a person can change not only to the good, but sometimes it happens that a person can change or be influenced to the bad and unethical.   Christian thought would back this up with its theory of temptation and the fallen angel, Satan.   I think most people would agree with me here, Detmar.

D: Haskell, you are right, and I also agree with you in that it may be possible that people can change for the bad although this type of thing would be hard to actually research and document scientifically.   As it is, I should only speculate about it, but human beings are not like cars where the driver can put it in reverse any old time.   Once a man's ethical makeup is established, it cannot be reversed to the un-ethical or anti-ethical easily if ever at all.

H: There are times when soldiers give up secrets or say things they should not.

D: That would be under duress or torture.   This situation of the human ethical makeup, a.k.a. conscience, is somewhat analogous   to   a   chemical   reaction.   Once   the   right understandings come about in youth, the ethical forms its ideas and as maturation proceeds so does the process of understanding the ethical.   The ingredients of the reaction are gathered by the situation and a reaction or understanding occurs.   To reverse this would be difficult just as it is with the chemical reaction.   If you take gasoline and oxygen and add a spark, you get a recombination of carbon dioxide, water, and heat. To reverse this chemical equation back to the gas and oxygen stage can only be done literally under great pressure. The soldier still has his ethical outlook but only under tremendous pressure is he forced to the unethical.

H: How about the spy who works for the other side of his own free will?   Is his objective and behavior unethical qualifying him as evil?

D: This may be your best example and probably it will be difficult to come to any conclusion. This is because if the spy does what he does due to his convictions that are aligned with the other side (the enemy), and if he believes that ultimately he is doing the world good and his objectives are good, this man is not evil. He may be wrong, and if caught, duly and properly punished, but he may not qualify as evil; we would consider him unethical. But I must qualify myself here in saying that his objectives must be absolutely good, not just good in his eyes. Hitler and Pol Pot may have thought that their objectives were good somehow. These objectives must be examined, and if they are not seen to be good then the spy would qualify as evil because in his endeavors he certainly also disrespected people directly or indirectly in his run toward his objective.

H: So the spy who worked for an opposing government whose interests are inimical to ours would be evil.

D: I assume you are speaking of a U.S. citizen, as a hypothetical example, working for the inimical foreign government because it makes a difference whose citizen it is.

The foreign citizen/spy was taught in his youth something different and his understanding of ethics may be quite different as he was not privileged to have our experiences and hence his loyalties are to another country.

H: But is it not that his and his country's objectives and methods are wrong and would that not make him, the foreign spy, evil?

D: No. Not evil. Unethical, yes.

H: Explain, please.

D: The foreign spy has been inculcated by his country to do certain things, usually to obtain stolen information, and therefore in our country his acts are unlawful. But to conclude the foreign spy is evil we need to show that he has unethical objectives and he is disrespectful and unethical in his methods of obtaining his objective. The foreign spy would defend himself by saying that he is endeavoring to bring peace to the world. If he was from a communist regime, he would say that through communism - or socialism - his and his country's efforts will bring justice, happiness, equality, utopia, or whatever to the world. He may truly believe that line of thought in which case he does not qualify as evil because justice, happiness, etc. are good objectives. Unfortunately, the fellow was deluded by his teachers, and if he lived in a country that upheld property rights, this spy's thoughts would change concerning how to achieve this better world.

H: But cannot we say that these things he has been taught are wrong?

D: Yes, we can. We can say that their view of the ethics of property rights is wrong. But our present subject is evil, and we need to conclude whether his objective is unethical. It is not enough to show that his system to bring about utopia is not of the good.

H: Then what about the spy who is of us, a U.S. citizen working for an inimical foreign government?Wouldn't he qualify as evil?

D: If he did his deeds for reasons such as sport, money, or excitement (all vanity), then certainly yes because they are selfish, unethical goals. If he did for reasons similar to the foreign spy, that is, if he felt what he was doing was for the benefit of the world as a whole and his true ideological beliefs were somehow as that of the foreign spy, then he might not be classified as evil. We would have to examine him in depth to really know.

H: But wait. It seems what you are saying is that as long as you feel that your goals are to benefit the world, then you can avoid being placed in the category of evil. What if Hitler or Pol Pot believed that what they were doing was ultimately good?   Probably they were self-deluded enough to actually think so. In that case, you would say that they are not evil? But, it is obvious that they are evil.

D: Yes, they are, of course. The difference is that it is not their thoughts of themselves that matter in the judgment of whether they are evil or not. This is our problem, and it is our historical judgment of their situation. We know the definition of evil, we know the standard by which evil is known and judged, and these people fit into that analysis. It doesn't matter if they are self-deluded megalomaniacs; we know that for whatever reason they instituted a pogrom, and a slaughter of the denizens of a society is anti-ethical. If someone's objective is genocide, then he is anti-ethical. We know that individual murder is against the ethical. It is universally understood that murder is wrong. It is in our conscience, in all societal laws, and in the principles of all religions. Hence, we know it to be an absolute in the nature of life because murder is anti-survival, therefore it is anti-ethical.

H: So why would not the spy be evil; isn't his objective anti-ethical in our view?

D: He may or may not be evil. It depends on our understanding of him and what he did. If we were to spend time to figure out his objective and purpose and examine his means to that end, we may or may not find him to be evil. It would be an easier question to examine his leaders about whom history may allow us to know more. A good question would be to explore other political figures to know if they fit our standard of evil or not.

H: I'm sorry; I still don't quite get it. Could you go over what is the difference between being evil and someone doing a wrong in a society, getting caught at the wrong, and being punished for the wrongful act that he committed against society?

D: Doing a socially wrongful deed is doing the unethical. As we explored earlier, ethics is the judgment of good and bad in behavior through the appropriate dispensation of respect, and if someone in society does something wrong, then it follows that that action is unethical. To live in society we accept the understanding that we must cooperate with each other, and acceptance of this cooperation between the individual and society in general and between the individual and the other individuals immediately around him, with those he comes into contact, and with those whom he deals in all the various ways that man interacts with the others in his society indicates sundry contracts, and the upholding of these understandings between men is justice. When one is caught at breaking one of these understandings, it is deemed a wrongful or unethical act and rectification of this wrongful deed and giving the men involved their Aristotelian due is called justice.

H: And evil?

D: Evil is the two-dimensional anti-ethical. The first dimension is at the individual level: a person constructs an anti-ethical objective; the second dimension is anti-societal behavior, to wit, the deployment of the means to its unethical end, and this necessarily involves the disrespect of others, and the substance of the disrespect is the anti-cooperative behavior against those that are in the way of the unethical objective.

H: I see. Thank you. This summary helps to make it clear. Let's get back to evil itself. I still have a problem accepting the relationship between the pure unadulterated evil we have seen in history and in some of the world's political leaders and our definition of evil. It seems the definition of evil, as we have it so far, describes what is unethical or even what might be a little bit evil, but it still, I feel, does not fit the pure real evil that has been seen in history. Your definition seems more appropriate to fit something like what is called an evil thought, or when we see a little boy do something pretty bad, we might describe him as "an evil little boy." The standard of evil explained is only two-dimensional, but perhaps real evil is three-dimensional, and I believe this third dimension is force. When the person uses force to attain his unethical objective and when this force is available to someone and he uses it to enforce his wrongful objective, he becomes evil, and when he uses a lot of force, he is really evil.

D: I see your point. The explanation is that our standard tells us that when the two parameters are fulfilled, evil makes its appearance. As in the example you just brought up about an evil thought, what makes it evil is the thought qualifying under the two unethical parameters. The thought has an unethical objective and the thought would be disrespectful to people if it were manifested, but as it remains a thought, it will be contained as just an evil thought. But that does not make the man evil, as a man is composed of many facets and he is a composite of many things. If the evil thoughts precipitate into actual attempts or completion of the unethical objects that were of the thoughts, then the evil grows in the reality of the person and we could say that person is evil. As for the magnitude of evil that he is, it would be due to the intensity of the unethical in both dimensions. The first dimension of the objective can be from an insignificant unethical aim as wanting to obtain another person's pen and appropriating it (deliberately) for one's own property. It's a little bit evil. It has the two dimensions: the unethical aim of obtaining the pen and the act of taking it which is the disrespect of another. Another example would be the dissembling of truth in communicating to another person with whom you are feigning cooperation to, say, obtain money surreptitiously. There is an unethical objective which might be the wish to obtain some money somehow, and the disrespect would be the actual transference of misinformation. It's the start of evil. The intensity of evil lies in the degree of the preponderance of the two unethical dimensions. Failing to give a greeting such as "good morning" is not as bad as failing to stop for a pedestrian and just mowing them over in a car or worse yet if you are a political leader and you initiate a pogrom. Hence, when we think of one of history's really evil ones, they possess the greatest degrees of anti-ethicality which is anti-survival which would be sending good people to their deaths, and the more people, the worse it is.

H: But I still feel that in order to be evil we need the third parameter to our standard of the capability of enforcement of the objective, that the evil one is empowered with the ability to apply his disrespect with impunity. That is, he may be evil in thought, but without the power to enforce his evil wishes (extremely unethical objectives), he is not evil in action. Hence, it seems to me that enforcement is the third parameter to our understanding.

D: You are without a doubt correct. You need to be able to accomplish the acts of disrespect in order to be considered evil in action, and this requires force and impunity from retribution because people often and eventually react to disrespect. Especially as the intensity and severity of the disrespect increases, people will not cooperate on their own accord with the disrespect. And hence, if you like, we could add this as a third parameter to the definition of evil, but I believe this aspect of the enforcement of or coercion to evil is inherent in the second ingredient of evil already.

H: How so?

D: The second parameter is the disrespect of the people that are in the way of the attainment of the objective (the first parameter) and completion or action of the disrespect implies that there is already the force to impel the action of the disrespect to completion and thus the evil is a fait accompli.

H: I see, and I think that I am coming to understand this problem of evil, but I still have a few questions yet. Why do you suppose there is evil? What do you suppose is its origin; whence does it come? Why do we have evil?

D: Yes, an interesting and perceptive interrogatory. First, let's consider the origin of the unethical in parameter two - the disrespect of others. In recalling yesterday's discussion we can easily know that the origin of disrespect is the non-cooperation with others and the source of non-cooperation is the ill-will consideration of another. The source for the first parameter of the anti-ethical objective where the evil one constructs a specific aim derives itself from the impulse of selfishness - complete, utter, self-involvement.

H: Wait. We are using the words "unethical" and "anti-ethical" interchangeably. Are they different?

D: Yes. The difference is that "unethical" just means that which is not ethical. But "anti-ethical" means that which is actively against survival; it is actively against respect and cooperation.

H: The complete selfishness of parameter two sounds like it is the same as the complete non-cooperation of parameter one. As I see it, the logical origin for non-consideration and non-cooperation would both be selfishness. As I recall, cooperation came from self-interest and the need to survive.

D: Yes, you are right. Complete, abject selfishness is the origin of both parameters as they both have ethicality as the prime ingredient. The perpetrator of evil somehow misses the connection between his self-interest and his singular self whether constructing some objective in which to channel his energies or in the inefficacy of disrespect of others. Somehow his self-involvement never breaks out of its shell and stays within itself to never recognize the value of others in one's society. This abject selfishness allows the evil one to be remorseless when dealing with others and blind to the sanctity of the social contracts amongst which he lives and should abide.

H: Although this makes sense and it seems logical that the ultimate source of evil should lie in abject selfishness, I cannot help but feel that this is a conjecture on your part. It seems that it would not stand up to professional scrutiny.

D: You're right. But the connection between selfishness and self-interest or survival seems close. I suggest that the evil one is an aberration of growth whereby the evil one cannot understand the difference between selfishness and self-interest within the confines of his evil circumstances and predicaments.

H: If by "self-interest" you mean the ability of the individual to recognize when cooperation with others is valuable to one's self, then I understand.

D: Yes.

H: Let's take an example or two. What about some of history's evil ones as we previously mentioned? Do you think their evil aims and horrible mistreatment of human lives had their origin in abject selfishness? Let's take Hitler or Pol Pot or any other of history's evil ones as an example.

D: I'm afraid we have gone as far as we can go without the assistance of worthies in the fields of psychology, psychiatry, politics, and theology. Once we work back to the origin of evil, we can go no further because the several disciplines just mentioned are needed to explain the aberrant psychological makeup objectives and the anti-ethical behavior of the evil ones. What makes the evil one veer from ethical self-interest to abject selfishness is subject to opinions of theologists or of psychologists who might say that some terrible event happened to him as a child and he grows up mentally malformed, to a geneticist who might proffer the suggestion that a behaviorally influential gene within the subject was mutant or that a deleterious rare allele has surfaced to cause the aberrant behavior.

H: So, in conclusion, evil arises when there are two parameters of the unethical objective and the aberrantly disrespectful appears toward those of the evil one's society. And as to the origins of evil and what impetus drives one to evil, we can only speculate that it derives itself in selfishness, but its specific causes which implant its seeds in the individual are not known by us for sure and we would have to search professional literature to see if there is any satisfactory answer available.

D: Yes. That's correct. It seems that there is a correlation between the unethical and selfishness, but the production of evil perhaps requires more. It is probably abject selfishness and self-corruption plus another ingredient like Satan or mutated genes, but we can only speculate. We can say that if one is devoid of selfishness, one cannot be unethical, and therefore, one cannot ever do evil.

H: Then it was impossible for Jesus to have done the unethical as he was devoid of selfishness and self-corruption.

D: Yes. Absolutely.

H: But what about misery? Is evil connected with misery, and why does it occur?

D: Misery is a by-product of the system of life that the creator established. Misery is an automatic by-product of the DNA-based life system. The creator set life in motion using DNA as its vehicle whereby energy from the sun is utilized by our DNA life system to run the whole show.

H: Are you telling me that misery cannot be eradicated from the face of the earth? If it is a natural by-product of life, then it will be constantly produced.

D: That's right. Science has and will reduce it further in the future, but it will always be produced.

H: Why? What's its nature?

D: Misery predominately appeared with the creation of the animal kingdom as it brought the advent of the DNA eaters. That is, animal DNA can only live by devouring other life. And when consciousness evolved, the cognizance of misery was realized and the awareness or the actual experience of misery was felt. In other words, misery occurs when there is unwilling sacrifice and sacrifice happens when one or more DNA cells are appropriated for another's use. When the sacrifice happens unwillingly, it produces misery. There is also a second type of misery. This is produced by natural disasters consequential to living on earth and being in the wrong place at the wrong time such as earthquakes, storms, or any event produced by force majeure. It is life's sacrifice for being on earth.

H: So I may take it that life is built on willing and unwilling sacrifices and it is the unwilling ones that produce the misery.

D: Correct. All life in the animal kingdom lives at the expense of other life as the animals 'DNA must have the assistance of other plant and/or animal DNA to live. You are well acquainted with the food chain, and fortunately, we humans, the Homo Sapiens, are at the top so we enjoy the least unwilling sacrifice of all, but at the same time, we are not immune to it.

H: But there are many different types of misery not just one animal being eaten by another.

D: Of course. But all the misery is sacrificial. Even the travails of a mother for her young are the sacrifice of her energy and time to provide production for her young. All non-pleasure is a kind of sacrifice.

H: Yes, in a sense you are right.

D: And when that which is unpleasant is done unwillingly, then it is done in misery. And the more unwillingly it is done, the more misery is involved.

H: What about the misery produced by evil? Evil-generated misery does not belong to the sacrificial system you just described, I think.

D: Misery that is produced by evil is, as we stated earlier, an aberration and is unnatural, but still the aberration is a part of the sacrifice for living in this world and is produced by probability.

H: I don't follow you.

D: There are two types of misery: the first is produced by the need for sacrifice to run this world. All production to run life is through some kind of sacrifice and most of it is willing sacrifice, but when it becomes unwilling sacrifice, it becomes misery.

H: Let me interrupt here. What about the child that is born deficient in some way and is miserable for it or some kid that is born in some slum and grows up hungry and in misery? How is this sacrificial?

D: This type of misery is of the same type that results from evil or the forces of earth and is of the second type. It is the general sacrifice of being human and having to live on this earth. Probability isn't kind to everybody. Some people will be unlucky and unfortunate to not be in the best circumstances. It is the unwilling sacrifice by life in specific for life in general to be alive on this earth. The real recipients are those that probability has blessed with the best circumstance and the least necessity for unwilling sacrifice.

H: If that is the way the world of life's behavior runs - on sacrifice - then how does one respond to the atheist's argument that given the existence of evil and misery, we can conclude that life is not perfect - but God is perfect - and therefore either God is not perfect or he does not exist because a perfect God could not create something imperfectly. That is, this system of DNA sacrifice and unwilling sacrifice unequivocally produces misery, and by just being on this earth by the sheer virtue of the law of probability whereby many times circumstances will be unfavorable to a significant portion of life in general and humans in particular, misery will occur. How can the theologian, apologist, or the Godly philosopher come to terms with this anomaly; how can he explain this problem of misery satisfactorily?

D: A great conundrum.

H: And we might as well add evil into this question also: how can the philosopher or theologian explain the existence of both evil and misery in this world?   How can there be coexistence between a perfect God and an imperfect world that includes misery and evil?

D: This answer may be a little surprising, but the world is as it is because it is perfect for us and we fit it perfectly.

H: You're right. I don't understand your statement at all. How can the inclusion of misery and evil into this world be deemed as a perfect world for us humans?

D: First, the world and the universe are ruled by natural laws that are perfect within themselves such as the laws of thermodynamics, Einstein's famous theories, Plank's constant, and others. Logic and reason that govern understanding are perfect things. The ways by which the universe operates are perfect.

H: I suppose so. Logic is perfect; I can understand that. Logic and reason are one hundred percent trustworthy. And I suppose the speed of light, Planck's constant et al are also perfectly reliable as far as our understanding goes. They may show up later should the "unifying theory" be discovered needing a slight adjustment just as Newton's theories were adjusted by Einstein. But in general, I suppose I could agree that the laws and forces that govern the universe are all perfectly reliable. The universe is not emotional; it is coldly rational and we humans are coming bit by bit to know and understand it. We are able to do this because the universe seems so far perfectly consistent with its own laws. Of course, we have not come to understand the workings of the laws that govern the universe perfectly yet, but we strive to do so. So far, we perceive that through the consistency of these mechanics, we can come to know quite a bit about the universe.

D: Yes. Because these workings of the world are perfectly consistent, they are perfect for our understanding and purposes.

H: I think I can agree so far. But continue, please, to explain how this world is perfect for us with the existence of misery and evil. I have my doubts about this, Detmar.

D: Yes. I understand. First, the origin of misery is sacrifice. As we mentioned, there is willing and unwilling sacrifice. With the willing sacrifice, I suspect that you don't have much problem. Although it is sacrifice nonetheless, it is willing and we choose to expend - usually - effort for the sake of something. We give up something of ourselves for something else. We go to work, expend effort, which is not fun, to get money to buy food so we can eat, live somewhere, buy a car, and do other things that are pleasurable to us (which by the way is the origin of the ethicalness of the free market). We make the sacrifice to reproduce progeny and expend the effort to raise them for the pleasure of having somebody to survive us.

H: Yes, I understand this much.

D: And the unwilling sacrifice, a great source of misery, is from being in the wrong unfortunate circumstances whereby one's sacrifices are greater than one would care to make in order to live. Or in the extreme case, one has to sacrifice his life for little or no reason other than to satisfy the laws of probability which indicate that so many people will die over time due to national disasters, sickness, accidents, et cetera.

H: Yes. Please proceed.

D: And the core of sacrifice is effort. Without effort, willing sacrifice is not possible.   That is, in order for an exchange to proceed to attain some desideratum, an effort is needed. With unwilling sacrifice, there is unwilling effort for an end that either is non-desirous or the end is not commensurate with our efforts of sacrifice and thus our efforts to this are undesirous and may even be reduced to little or none.

H: OK.

D: In order for us to proceed with effort (production) we need to have the means to assess the deployment of effort, and this is free will. Free will employs reason, emotional desires, biological impulses, feelings, and other internal originating experiences in assessing our situation. This situation about which a decision is to be made has inherent in it a factor of risk. There is risk and free will in every decision that we make. We freely evaluate the risk involved and use the engine of free will to choose.

H: I have a feeling that you are correct here about risk being present in our decisions, but I am wondering whether it is always present.

D: Yes. Without risk, the assessed situation would be one hundred percent certain, and since nothing in our diurnal, physical lives is absolutely certain, risk in our daily decisions is always present at least to some degree. The nature of the risk and uncertainty is that we wonder whether we will receive an expected amount of return for our efforts. It is in this return that lies the risk.

H: Does this cover every type of decision that we make?

D: Yes. Even in walking across the street or eating some food or whatever. If we are about to walk across the street (the effort) to get to the other side of the street where there is a restaurant which is our destination (return on effort), there is a risk that in walking across the street we will not make it or that to do it may require too much effort. Even when faced at a restaurant with what to choose for dinner, we must make the choice between one type of food or another for which we will pay money (money - which represents production - being the consequence of effort) and this choice is replete with risk because the food may come out poorly done, or the service may not be satisfactory, or we may not receive as much food as we expect. There is always some unknown factor in what we do, and ergo, the element of risk appears.

H: OK, so there are these interrelated factors of risk, freewill, effort, and sacrifice. But what is the significance of it all? How does any of this relate to justifying the existence of misery in this world?

D: Because we must have in our lives, in order to be attuned with ourselves, the free will to assess the risk of sacrificing our efforts for some pleasurable return, and because this system of free will and risk assessment is not perfect and there are mistakes, misery appears.

H: Still, I feel I do not understand yet. So what if we do not have these ingredients in our world? If the system of the world were changed to a perfect one, whatever that may be, it seems that in this hypothetical perfect world, misery would be absent: that would be great. And so what, that one or more of these ingredients in our present world would be lacking or changed or whatever?

D: These ingredients are impossible to change and leave the world and us in any way even similar to how we are. Probability dictates that it is impossible to completely eliminate misery. Misery is, as the laws that govern this universe, perfect within itself, and misery is requisite to our happiness.

H: What? Are you saying that the inclusion of misery in the world is requisite to our temporal happiness?

D: Yes. It is. And I will explain.

H: This will be interesting, Detmar.

D: The key component in life's behavior is free will. We must and should have free will. If you were an atheist I think you would agree that we necessarily need free will to operate our lives, and if you consider the creation of the universe by God, we need free will to operate in general our lives.

H: Why the qualification?

D: I say that "in general" we need free will if we have religious faith because there might be divine revelation or intervention occasionally in some people's lives that would, if it were to happen, preclude free will for that particular extent of the intervention.

H: Do you mean that during that time were God to bring into one's life some revelation or intervention, free will would be absent?

D: Yes.

H: Why?

D: The answer will come out in a little bit. To continue, free will is needed to make us individuals capable of living in this world. Once free will is present, it necessarily invokes the presence of choice and the assessment of the risk of choice. Incumbent with choice is the effort to attain the choice which means sacrifice, and of course, if there is choice there is risk assessment.

H: Cannot we have sacrifice, effort, and free will without risk?

D: No. It is impossible. If there is free will and the freedom to choose one thing over another or do one thing instead of another exists, then the absence of risk is impossible.

H: Why?

D: The absence of risk is impossible even in a perfect world such as this one because there is assessment of choice to one thing over another and that necessarily makes risk incumbent to the situation because even though the choice may be between good things, if assessment is involved, it cannot be a perfect situation. A choice between two or more perfect things cannot happen. If it is a choice, then one thing is not equal in the same way to the other and assessment is involved.

H: So if there is free will, there is choice, and hence risk.

D: Yes. And if there were no risk in the universe and everything is perfect, then there could be no freedom of choice and free will. And if there would be no free will and everything would be perfect, then sacrifice would cease to be (and hence, misery would cease to be). But this is impossible for us as a no-risk universe means that we cannot make decisions freely without limitations. We would be able to do anything inhibited only by our physical being, this being a limitation in itself and thus subject to risk. So in order to eliminate risk completely, we would need to eliminate even our physical bodies. So unless we rid ourselves of all universal risk and our own personal physical selves, we cannot eliminate risk and hence, misery altogether. If we were to eliminate risk altogether, there would be no physical us, no universe. We would have to be perfect to exist and this is impossible because only God can be perfect and exist. Hence, for the human world and life in general risk is a necessary incumbency.

H: I see, somewhat. Well, what if we had risk but did not have one of the other ingredients that we have been talking about like free will, effort, or sacrifice?

D: It would again be impossible. If no free will, then either we do not make our own choices and somebody makes them for us, or we no longer have the ability to make any choices in which case we do not make any choices and thereby cannot live, or God would have to make all our choices in which case we would be living by divine revelation or intervention all the time. Finally, in order to avoid misery, if there were no effort or sacrifice on our part, but yet there is risk and free will, we would have to have everything done for us. We could do nothing for ourselves in case it was the wrong thing and misery might result.

H: Then, it is impossible all around to have a universe without misery or at least the probability or potential for misery to occur.

D: Yes, we are not perfect. Only that which can avoid risk can be perfect. And if the divine were to create a world for life, then unless that life were also divine, misery will be an incumbency for that world.

H: I see. How about evil? Could evil only be eliminated from this world and leave misery by itself?

D: Evil is part of misery. Misery is generated from unwilling sacrifice of which there can be evil as evil necessitates unwilling sacrifice. Recalling our understanding of evil, evil is unethical behavior with an unethical objective. As there is resistance to unethical objectives, unethical behavior requires the use of physical force or mental guile to obtain its objective over its unfortunate subjects. Evil differs from unethical behavior in that it is two-dimensional - the unethical behavior along with the wrongful objective. Thus, in order to eliminate evil we need to eliminate one of the two parameters. But to eliminate a dimension of evil we need to eliminate one of the factors that make up its behavior in order to prevent the individual from doing either the unethical behavior or creating the anti-ethical objective. Unfortunately, any modification would mean modification to free will, and good or bad, free will is necessary to life's system in the universe.

H: But it seems to me that evil is so unnecessary and that when it appears, it can be so destructive. Looking at history, I sadden at all the misery, all the useless sacrifice that has been made by people when the awful evil appears and takes hold. Such pogroms in Africa, Asia, and Europe were sickening, and I guess I would like to see some hope of its elimination even if I could not do something physical about it, except perhaps by appeal through prayer if I thought it would help.
D: Much of evil can be prevented politically. Society can choose methods to prevent it from surfacing. But

unfortunately, it cannot be eliminated on a small individual scale because of the free will problem.

H: Well, at least how do we rid ourselves of it on the grand scale? I assume you are speaking on the political scale as this is where history's great evil has lurked.

D: Right.   As you know there are several types of government such as totalitarianism, oligarchy, and democratic republics.   When governmental power in whatever form begins to make wrongful or inept decisions, things start to deteriorate if the government has much political power. If the government has limited power, the decisions do not have as far-reaching consequences.   The potential for problems to begin is when political power is concentrated and unrestrained.   If ineptness or evil seeps into concentrated political power such as a totalitarian government which would have few restraints and is ruled by only one person, the potential for misery is great. If the single, unrestrained ruler has a penchant for evil, then misery will ensue. And I believe this has been the case for almost all the political evil pogroms in the world.

H: Has not democracy caused any evil?

D: Only very small portions compared to the totalitarian states.

H: Why do you suppose? Is there some inherent factor within democracy that provides an inhibiting factor to the encroachment of evil?

D: Yes.   First, democracies tend to have restrained governments; secondly, because governmental power comes under periodic review by its constituencies, it generally seeks ethical objectives. As people base their behavior on survival, in general people prefer ethical behavior and ethical objectives. Thus, evil has had a hard time in developing in democracies, although it has appeared in small doses here and there on a relatively minor scale.   When the democratic society realizes an unethical objective with the appearance of evil, they have and do squash for the most part the wrongful actions and objective.

H: I think I can agree with you in general.   But I'm curious because nothing comes to mind that clearly qualifies as evil actions in the democratic republics that I can think of. Even our involvement in the Vietnam Era does not qualify because although it could be argued that we did many unethical things there, it seems that our goal or objective was not unethical. I believe we did have some sort of lofty idea of protecting the people of South Vietnam from communism. So I am curious about what you are thinking of with regard to evil in democratic governments. Of course, you may be thinking of Hitler as he was elected under a democratic situation, but after he got into office, he declared an emergency and under the articles of the German constitution he usurped ultimate control of the government from the people on spurious pretexts.

D: Some evil actions, where a concentration of power in the hands of a few or one for a short period of time without review or restraint, can occasionally happen on a limited scale in democracies because it's difficult to have democratic oversight over every governmental action. Examples can occur when these circumstances arise, although they certainly do not necessarily happen. But nevertheless, occasionally an unethical action with an unethical objective can occur. An example of this was the forced repatriation of refugees after World War II to a devastating lethal totalitarian regime. Another would be the unethical actions of law enforcement against private citizens without due or probable cause. Examples of this occasionally happen here in the U.S., but to go deeper into this would be to get off the path of our present inquiry as we should keep to the theory of ethics and avoid an embarkation on historical polemics.

H: Then I believe I have finished my questions regarding evil. I would, now, like to get back to ethics proper and ask about some problems and examples of ethics.

D: That would be fine. I suggest that we take a break until later.

H: That would be fine. I'll drop by tomorrow again in the early afternoon.

D: I look forward to it.

H: Thanks very much, Professor, for today's conversation and time. It was interesting.

D: See you tomorrow.

H: OK. Good-bye.

Chapter 4

Applied Ethics

Haskell, the next day, reappears at the office of Detmar in the mid-afternoon when he knows Detmar is most likely to be in. Tapping the open door he announces himself and at Detmar's bidding walks in.

H: Thank you, Detmar, for yesterday's discussion. It was most interesting and as we digressed quite a ways away from the original inquiry of ethics and judgment and proceeded into evil, sacrifice, and misery, I would like to get back to ethics.

D: All right. Shoot.

H: Today, I would like to see if we can use what we have so far discussed to understand what is ethical and not ethical with regard to some perplexing fundamental problems.

D: Such as?

H: Well, we began to touch upon such basic issues yesterday when we discussed in what way democracy is better than totalitarian governments. I would like to continue with such topics. One that is very fundamental in society is whether there should be property rights or not. That is, what is more ethical: communal ownership of resources (communism) or a society that permits individual property ownership (a free market society or capitalism), or something in between like a state that allows free markets but heavily taxes them for entitlement purposes. This heavy taxation, of course, essentially would be a kind, or degree, of communal ownership.

D: Yes, for the most part, especially where entitlements and government social welfare is concerned, taxation is spreading to community members resources generated by others. However, we must remember that government arguably may have some purposes by which they are useful in the service of the people and perform these services more efficiently than society. An example of that could possibly be the defense of the country.

H: Yes. I agree. But what, would you say, is the most ethical form of economics?

D: First, we must remember that ethics is the study of good and bad in behavior and that the good and bad are based on the coefficient of survival of society.

H: Yes. We learned that.

D: So the basis of how we should judge whether an economic system is better than another is to use the standard that promotes the survival or betterment of society. We have found of late that it is eminently true by empirical evidence that a free market society is more efficient than those that are based on communism as we have seen the dissolution of the former Soviet Union which practiced oligarchic totalitarian socialism/communism where individuals could not own much property and the markets were officially not open ones.

H: Yes. But is one inherently better or more ethical than the other?

D: For the most part, yes, but not in every case.

H: How so? Applying our standard of ethics cannot we say that a free market capitalism is more ethical as we have seen that it is more efficient at promoting the overall betterment of society in general?

D: Yes, we can say that in general, but it needs a qualification because it is not the most efficient nor does it promote survival the most in every case. It appears that in significant societies that possess agriculture and technology, the free market with property rights is eminently the best. But in small, primitive, tribal societies, property rights are limited, and it seems from anthropological texts that communistic type societies appear as long as the societies remain very small and primitive.   If these small societies work well with their communal type economy, then it would be more ethical to have this type of economic system than any other in small primitive groups.

H: So, if we know by whatever evidence that one type of economic system is better than another for a society, then that system is the ethical one.

D: Yes.

H: And I suppose that this would be true for government as we discussed. Democracy is a better system because we know that it is best at preventing evil from occurring in the political arena.

D: Yes. But if we could be assured somehow that a different type of government such as a monarchy or Plato's government by elitist philosophers would be immune from evil and could at the same time carry on government functions and execution of the laws of the society generation after generation, then these other forms of government would be fine. But there is no assurance, and history confirms they do not. There can be no assurance due to the existence of risk. Only democracy provides this assurance because people want that which will seem to them good and that which will promote their own particular well-being and survival. And if taken collectively, the general sense of what is wanted in the behavior of the government is known over time. And hence, there is an inherent check against perpetual evil and long-term bad decisions.

H: I see. So in anything that we do or decide, if it is efficacious to our survival, then it is ethical.

D: Almost. We must remember that ethics does not exist relative to only one person. Ethics requires society. So what is efficacious to the survival of society is that which is ethical.

H: All right. Then, how do we make personal ethical decisions?

D: We make ethical decisions by choosing that which is respectful. When we consider the other people that our decisions concern, then we are choosing the ethical. So if a decision presents itself to us and it does not concern very many people, then its ethical importance is slight in scale and we must only think of those that our decision concerns.

However, if we were the president of the United States, our decisions concern many. In order to be ethical in our decisions we must try to be respectful to the most people that we can. In other words, we must do that which most furthers the survivability of the country as ethics is based on the survival of society. The vehicle by which ethics critiques its decisions is by respect. The president must be respectful to those whom his decisions influence; that is, he must consider the people to whom the consequences of his decision extend. He must try to favorably extend these consequences of his decisions as much as possible, and the survivability of the U.S. society will increase (as long as his reasoning and thinking are correct). But if he doesn't make the right decisions and the survivability of society seems to be declining in the minds of those voting members of the country's constituency who have come to feel that the influence of his decisions has been negative overall, they will eventually replace him with somebody else who they perceive will do a better job at making the right decision that will increase the survivability of their society.

H: Hence, the president is ethical as long as he is trying to make the decision which has the most good for the U.S. society.

D: Yes.

H: Sounds right out of the utilitarian handbook.

D: Yes.

H: Is that which is utilitarian the creed of the ethical?

D: Basically, in a private sense, yes. When we make our ethical decisions, we consider those around us who are involved, and the more influential and weighty the consequences of the decision are, the more one must consider those involved.

H: But what if the decision concerned is one that involves much good for oneself and much bad for many others?

D: Fortunately, this situation does not happen in the private sector of societies. Unfortunately, it mostly occurs in the political arena under the banner of ideology whether it be war based on a grab for more political territory, or to quell a territory that is against the political and/or economic policies of a political entity, and so on.

H: How do we know if a political leader makes an ethical decision in this case of starting a war or anywhere there is a leader who knows there is going to be a lot of misery, death, tragedy, hardship, and so on as an outcome of his decision?

D: If he is an ethical leader, he will base his decision on what is best overall for his country as he perceives the situation. If he is unethical, then his objective will be suspect and not in accordance with the good of his countrymen. He will have a private agenda that may clash with the public welfare and here in this instance, he would become unethical. And this private separate decision is selfish because it does not take into account his countrymen's welfare and it is selfish in that it is driven by either a personal wealth motive or a personal ideological decision. Again, this situation will most likely occur only in a non-democratic situation.

H: When would it be ethical for a revolution to occur? That is, when can a populous rebel and wage war or seek revenge against a sitting government? I suspect you will say that it is when a populous sees that a sitting government is not acting in accordance with its interests?

D: Basically, this is correct. Rebellions may ethically take place not only when a constituency's interests are ignored over time, but especially when the populous is abused undeservedly.

H: You mean any time a person becomes unhappy for some reason they can legitimately rebel against a government. It seems kind of whimsical.

D: Yes. Any time. But a populous is slow-moving and deliberate, and it takes a while to rile a significant body of people. An individual is more quick to react to some injustice done to him and that is why revolutions are fomented by certain individuals who are incensed and then rally others to a purpose and eventually to a rebellion. During all this time the government must be significantly oppressive in order to keep up the grist for the fomenter's mill of producing revolutionaries who hold his line of thinking. It is rare indeed to see a whole body of people who suddenly rise violently against a government and dissolve it. If that were to happen, we can safely say that the sitting government would have to have been extremely oppressive, violent, and totally inconsiderate of its populous. But such political bodies usually are aware of their own ill will and inconsideration of their constituents and would take steps such as disarming the people and forming secret police to prevent any uprising from occurring.

H: Yes, that seems consistent with what I know of revolutions, but it seems that there is another situation of rebellion we have not covered and that would be where a society is not oppressed and there is a considerate government in place but through a different political ideology a rebellious leader appears and tries to overthrow a government. Can this ideologically driven rebel be an ethical individual?

D: This is simply an ideologue with a conflicting philosophy and he believes he is right, and his trying to conscript others into his camp of beliefs and ideas is fine. In fact, the free availability to a society of information and ideas is healthy to a society as the founders of the U.S. knew and their addition of the First Amendment to the Constitution exemplified.

H: Actually, I was thinking of the rebellious, ideologically driven leader who uses violence against his considerate government. Especially those revolutionaries that hold to the maxim that the overthrow should be done by any means availableand their violent approach is justifiable. These people believe that the end justifies the means.

D: I see. No, they are not ethical, but despicable and probably evil. Should a revolutionary not be able to garner many followers through his propagandizing, but proceed to violence directly against a government that is non-oppressive, free, without secret police, and should he commit harm to people and property, he will have an unethical objective and use unethical actions qualifying him as evil.

H: But what if he feels that his objective is good; it is just that nobody else does, and he feels that for the good of mankind, he must bring on the revolution whether the people are with him or not?

D: It does not matter whether he believes that what he is doing is right or not. If there is protection for his free speech in that society, he has the time to make converts to his ideology. Therefore, if the government is not persecuting him and his group with violent means and has allowed free speech and sanctity of contract (both social and individual), then the government is considerate of him, and violent overthrow is not ethical. And in addition, it is evil because even if in his mind he believes truly in what he is doing and that it is right, his objective has within it not only the change of government but also the objective of destruction or transference of private property, and often these types wreak havoc, destroy lives, and disseminate misery. And if their only justification for this is that the end justifies the means, they are wrong and evil.

H: I see. So the key point here is if the society is free, and free speech is permitted, and the government is not seeking the banishment of the revolutionary for his ideas, he does not have any ethical foundation to prosecute his ideas with violence.

D: Yes. That's correct.

H: So, the primary way a government is considerate of the constituency is by protecting free speech and upholding private and social contracts.

D: And allowing redress of government through political means. As we have already noted, democracy provides the most favorable means for this. There may be another form of government that may provide for equitable redress of government by the people and public opinion, but I am not aware of it. Perhaps Plato's philosopher elites may qualify, but among even these over time only democracy will prevent the control of government from falling into unethical hands for extended periods of time and perpetually provide for continual redress and review of government.

H: I agree. Well, what about an individual in society who is miserable, he may or may not have an ideology for or against the system, and he is lacking adequate sustenance and accommodation due to his unfortunate circumstances - is he still an ethical person if he breaks a law to obtain provisions by stealing? If a man is desperate what can he do?

D: Ethics is based on survival. If there is no means by which a man can cooperate with others to obtain mere sustenance as he must survive, he wouldn't be unethical if he proceeded to appropriate the basics without violence and harm to others.

H: What about stealing? Should he be allowed to steal and yet still be considered ethical?

D: Yes, to the extent that the desperate's stealing is of a quantity that does not have a deleterious effect on the possessor's food life's necessities and the objects of the perpetrator do not exceed that which is elementary and necessary to his existence.

H: But your word "deleterious" is too nebulous and could be understood to mean almost any quantity of the purloined goods by the needy. For example, it would be easy to show that even against the rich just the taking of a loaf of bread is deleterious to the wealthy one in some way. Let's suppose the wealthy one would say that stealing detracts from his overall wealth and thus it has a negative effect.

D: Yes, you are right. If property rights are declared necessary in the society of the wealthy one and the mendicant, then they need to be protected. But the society must recognize the need of the mendicant to survive. So the only way to be able to solve this problem is to interrogate the contracts that dictate and enumerate the rights of both parties.

H: OK. Proceed.

D: In the eyes of the indigent either there is no contract with society or if there were, it is abrogated due to lack of cooperation. If he has truly tried to earn a living but cannot for whatever reason and has become poor, he will feel that there is no social contract in place, and just in order to survive he knows that he may have to break a rule of society. Society's view, of course, is that it must protect itself and the system that it has set up including the system of property rights and it will try to prevent transgressions of its rules.

H: So should the mendicant be allowed to steal?

D: Society's view will be that stealing is not allowed. The mendicant's view is that he has no choice. He says to himself that I must steal; I am alone in this world in that I cannot receive any cooperation. It is obvious both sides have a point and it looks like the twain shall not meet or be able to compromise. However, although society has its hard and fast rules, it must take into account discrepancies such as this example where the understandings of the in-place contract break down. In this case, it should be recognized that the mendicant acted unethically in society's view; in his own view, his actions were compulsory and were a-ethical. He knows that society will view it as unethical, and if he would like to comply, but cannot, then society has to look at his point of view of the contract, or lack of contract, and his situation and become lenient.

H: By "lenient" you mean that society should forgive the mendicant transgressor.

D: If not wholly, it should in some part due to the circumstances. And our society does this quite a bit now and there is a vehement argument going on whether it is being done to too great an extent or not.

H: I see. So when a transgression is done due to circumstances that render this perpetrator to compulsively transgress society's rules, leniency should be considered due to the breakdown of the possible lack of cooperation on both sides of the social contract.

D: That is correct. And this recognition of the mitigating circumstance of the social breakdown of the cooperation of both parties should be recognized and therefore leniency invoked.

H: And I take it that leniency is then the determination that requirements of a contract do not have to be performed.

D: Yes, leniency is the non-requisite fulfillment of a contractual cooperative relationship.

H: Yes. Well, I would like to get back to what you have been saying here about the revolutionary and the individual actions one can take against a government and that it makes sense about the ethical being as the utilitarian slogan says, the most good for the most people. But I am not putting it all together yet so that I have an integrated understanding of it all. I think that what I need is an explanation of what should be the relationship between the individual. society and government. What is the ethical, equitable situation for the individual man and society? I believe that we cannot have as our only guide to the laws of a society that which is the greatest good for the most people. I feel that this would neglect the importance of the individual, and I believe in the rights of the individual amidst a society as we, in America, have protected and enumerated in the Bill of Rights in the form of amendments to the Constitution.

D: You are right. The individual needs to be protected.

H: How do we do this and yet be consistent with our utilitarian maxim? What are the understandings that should exist between man and society in order to asseverate that the relationship is ethical for both? In other words are there any inherent, a priori rights that dictate the relationship?

D: By our standard for ethics we know that all ethics is based on survival and that ethics, itself, is how to cooperatively behave in society through the appropriate dispensation of respect, and, of course, it can include how a government behaves toward the individual as dictated by its laws and by the behavior of its agents. The individual's actions must reflect respect which indicates cooperation to attain the status of good and ethical behavior.

H: Yes, I recall.

D: Along with this standard we can understand that there are two parameters to the ethical in the relationship of man to society. First is that the individual must be able to exist before he can cooperate with others to the benefit of furthering society. The second phase is the individual interacting and cooperating with others. Therefore, the individual has the ethical right to exist, survive, and interact. Once he is able to survive and interact, society has the ethical right to demand that the individual cooperates with society to further its survival. All subsequent rules, laws, and understandings must have their basis in this basic relationship otherwise it - the laws, regulations, or individual's behavior - would be unethical.

H: Are there any fundamental concepts that develop from this basic tenet of ethics of the individual's right to promote his own survival and society's demand for cooperation to further its own existence, such as free speech, property rights, sanctity of contract, and self-defense? If a society did not have these rules to govern itself, would the society be unethical?

D: Good question. Yes, in order to promote survival for all individuals a society must respect the sanctity of the individual and hold it important because without individuals there can be no society.   Therefore, the sanctity of the individual or respect of the individual must be overt.   Such respect would be demonstrated by society's understanding that there shall be no murder or violence by society toward its constituents. For the individual to survive that person will necessarily need to communicate to others, and so society needs to have the sanctity of communication; also in order to cooperate, society will need the sanctity of understanding also known as the sanctity of contracts. These types of rules of society have already been discussed, clarified, and justified by many before us.   The justification and necessity of these ethical rules have been delineated and elaborated already in the Bible, in the U.S. Constitution with its Bill of Rights, and by philosophers such as Locke and Adam Smith, and also by more recent economists such as Friedman and others. All of them have developed systems that purport what is best for society. Our purpose here was to discover the origin and content of such ethical understandings or societal laws that have already been laid down for us.

H: I see. Then to summarily iterate our conclusion, all ethical laws, regulations, rules, and behavior must conform to the respect of the individual to protect him in order to insure his survival which is necessary in order to ensure the health of society in general, and secondly, society's rules can demand the cooperation of the individual constituents to further the cohesiveness of society and hence, its overall survival. Rules that counter these two fundamental principles would be unethical.

D: Precisely. And although we advocate the utilitarian creed, we do so only with the understanding that the optimum good has two parameters: the respect of the individual and society's need for cooperation. This combination will bring the most good for the most people.

H: I understand. Let's go to a question that is much discussed nowadays. With our present understanding of ethics being fairly well developed I would be curious to hear your opinion about abortion.

D: Hot topic.

H: Yes. I think I know at least partially what you will say.

D: Go ahead.

H: If we take our standard for ethics, abortion is clearly unethical except when the mother's life is in some sort of danger or physical compromise, such as rape, as it is not furthering the survival of society.

D: Good. It is eminently clear that abortion is for the most part not based on survival. One characteristic of the abortion of a pregnancy is that the pregnancy is inconvenient to the female's time of life; for instance, she is out of wedlock; not yet finished with school, etc., and this is a selfish point of view. The reasoning is that she owns her own body, the pregnancy is ill-timed and unwanted; at another time she can devote herself to procreating, therefore she can end the pregnancy and be within her rights, her rights being that which is described by the laws put down by our society.

H: I get the impression that it may be ethical?

D: If the woman were a victim and became pregnant in an unwilling event and was violated, then she can argue that the pregnancy is an unethical violation of her body and the fetus is repugnant to her. As she has a repugnant burden that may be a perpetual mental irritant, and it may affect her life adversely, it could be viewed as not an unethical act to terminate the pregnancy. Also, if the fetus endangers the survival of the mother, it is also clear that a termination is not an unethical act as it is clear that the survival of the mother has been affected.

H: Perhaps we could call it an a-ethical act.

D: Yes. And if it is a case of inconvenience and her situation came by a consentaneous act, she may argue that although of consent, it was a mistake and by terminating the pregnancy, it will allow her to procreate later when a more efficacious time develops as the present time would not be as good a time due to some reason perhaps say that she has not finished school. She could argue that at a later time, she could give greater attention to a family or that her present mate isn't willing to be a father and without a father, it would not be the best time to bring up a family. And so, it could be argued that an aborted pregnancy is not necessarily anti-survival especially considering her intention on procreating and raising a family; it just happens that it is not the optimum time and circumstances.

H: So, I take it that although we cannot call abortion an unethical act, it appears that it may be just an a-ethical act.

D: Well, let's follow it all the way through. Ethics, we know, is based on survival, but also it has the component of cooperation manifested by the vehicle of respect. Ethics is respect for the sake of facilitating cooperation so society can survive and flourish. The termination of a pregnancy is an act of utter disregard and disrespect for the fetus, the unborn potential child.

H: And therefore unethical. But, of course, although it is an unethical act against a fetus, we need to come to the determination if the unborn is a person. One side says that it is not a person, but just part of the woman's body especially during the early pregnancy. And the other argument is that although not developed yet, it has the potential to become a full human being and should be accorded the rights of one. But where does anyone draw the line? At birth, the child has the potential to become a grown-up. At conception, the fertile egg has the potential to become a baby and then an adult. The potential is present everywhere; so where can anyone draw the line and say when it is ethical or not to have an abortion?

D: As we discussed before, there are two parameters to the nature of ethics. First, an individual has an interest in existing and surviving, and it is bound by its free will to try to exist and survive. It is absolutely fundamental to life that we respect the sanctity of our own lives first, that we grant ourselves the right, or at least the option, to live and survive. The secondary component is that we interact for the purpose of ensuring and furthering our own survival and the lives of our progeny and this interacting is accomplished by cooperating with others using the vehicle of respect. Hence, we need to accept that there is an absolute need to cooperate with others and this cooperation is the foundation of ethics.

H: Yes. We have covered this. And we know that abortion is an unethical disrespectful (uncooperative) act, to say the least, against the unborn, but do we have an ethical incumbency to cooperate with a fetus and at what stage does it become ethically incumbent upon us to cooperate with the unborn and foster its growth into a new human being? At first, it is only a single fertile cell, but within a short period of time it becomes differentiated and its potential ontogenetic development is a harbinger of a future person.

D: Obviously, to abort a pregnancy becomes more ethically taboo as the development of the unborn proceeds, but right from inception it is an unethical action to interdict the biological proceedings except as we have noted. As every cell appears, as the growth occurs, the interdiction becomes a greater unethical action. Nevertheless, even against the first single fertile cell, uncooperative action is undeniably unethical. However, there are circumstances whereby the start of a life may be shrouded in unethical circumstances of which justice may permit rectification, and it would be unfortunate if this process includes misery for the unborn, but as we have discussed due to free will and the nature of our surroundings misery is sometimes unavoidable, and although we humans throughout the world are working hard to reduce the amount of misery present, and I believe are overall succeeding at this task, still there are times when misery is unavoidable.

H: Yes.

D: Fortunately, pregnancy is usually a premeditated and joyful event. However, sometimes it is not. And if not, the consideration of an interdiction against the developing unborn must take into account that the action is unethical. However, if the situation of the pregnancy has unethical antecedents a decision to abort is not unethical. If the impregnator was not in violation of ethical precedents, but it is a matter of some inconvenience whereby the pregnancy would be better at another time, the unethicalness of the action against the unborn must be weighed against the misery factor in one's life. If the misery brought on by the birth of progeny is extreme and will affect greatly the life of the parents, the shift of the misery to the unborn can understandably occur, but it must be a real and not frivolous rationalization because in today's world children are often sought after by infertile parents which seek adoption of children and so real and true misery based on inconvenience is at best rare. Hence, abortion of a pregnancy for inconvenient purposes in today's world can rarely be an action that is not unethical.

H: So as I understand it, abortion is never ethical if we consider it alone as a singular, particular situation. However, if it has related circumstances that involve the consequences of misery, it can be justified to the extent that it is not unethical.

D: And in order to justify an abortion there must be a preponderance of misery to outweigh the respect that we must garner for human life and the potential development of the life.

H: Yes. That brings me to ask why is there such a dichotomy between those"pro-choice" people who favor abortion on demand and the "pro-life" who are against the termination of pregnancies. There seems to be quite a disparity in each point of view, and I am wondering why this is.

D: It is because of the amount of respect that each accords the life of the unborn. One side indicates that no respect is due because it is something that is not yet developed, and its potential for development into a human being is discounted completely.

H: I see. And the other side attributes great respect to the unborn and its potential for development. It is the attribution of respect that creates the dichotomy. One side cannot understand why the other should treat the initial life without respect.

D: Also, one should consider that there is a derivative of this significant allocation of respect to the unborn. This derivative is from an understanding that life has a purpose and we are here because we were caused to be here, and hence life is special, especially human life, and should be held extremely importantly, and to void it is a weighty decision and should only be done under the most extreme situations. The pro-choice advocates are probably not as concerned with this sanctity of life at any stage of development. They probably become more concerned with the life of the unborn as it develops toward full term.

H: Is there a right stance?

D: If you know how much God wants us to treat life and its potential for development, which I would hazard to say is great, then we have a position to consider life of the unborn at whatever the stage as extremely dear and important, and termination of the unborn should be weighed only against a factor of the dispensation of misery. As misery is something in this world that we must work to alleviate, where there is significant misery attendant to a pregnancy, termination can be considered, but it must be significant and preponderant misery for termination to be ethical.

H: I see. Sometimes we hear in these types of discussions about the "rights" of the unborn or for that matter rights of most anything - right to work, right to a job, natural rights, and so on. I remember that we briefly discussed what a right is. As I recall it, a right is a contractual understanding, but that does not quite fit these cases as I see it. How is the right to work, the right to a job, or for that matter the rights of the unborn, related to understandings within a contract?

D: If there is no contract, there is no right. If a person declares that he has the right to a job then he must explain that there is a contract in force somewhere. I suppose the person who would declare that such a right exists would have to explain that there is a contract between him and his adherents to this view and the commercial industrial society in which he lives. Or possibly, he believes that there is a contract current between him and a government, and this government can by conscription provide private sector employment or offer government employment, or possibly he might think that there is a secondary contract between the government and the private sector to provide the employment. But in any case without the contract, there exists no right. In this case about the right to a job, there actually is probably not a contract in effect and hence, no actual right to a job.

H: I see. How about when they talk about the rights of the unborn? Where is the contract?

D: Perhaps some would say that there is no contract at all, and thus there are no rights integral to the unborn. But others would say that a contract automatically comes in force when two consenting adults conjugate to create a fertile egg. The resulting embryo automatically relies on the mother to gestate on its behalf and bring the unborn into the world. It is an implied contract because I exist by your own doing, I will rely on you as you will cooperate and bring me to term; I will be your progeny and survive you; you will give me life.

H: Some people do not take this seriously.

D: That's true, and if they do not, then they will not attribute any rights to the unborn.

H: Do the unborn have rights? What is the answer?

D: The essence of a right, we know, exists within the contract. When a child is conceived by one's own volition, a contract appears between parents and the unborn. At first the unborn is tiny, undifferentiated, physically not much. It is mostly potential. With each passing day, the physicalness becomes more, and the potential less, and consequently the contract becomes more manifest, real, and of the moment. The unborn accrues its rights as the contract matures and its pith solidifies and becomes real. The unborn has rights and the rights are commensurate with the contract in force at conception; and as the unborn develops with each passing day, the contract and thusly, the rights of the unborn become stronger and more obvious because with each passing day, the implied contract becomes more apparent and overt. Hence, at first, the initial fertilized egg has an in place contract and to abrogate it takes an invocation of the misery factor and with each passing day, the contract becomes stronger and more manifest and to break, it requires a greater degree of misery.

H: Well, what about an environmentalist? When he talks about the rights of animals or a species that has become endangered, it seems dubious to me that there exists a contract, and thus, a right of the animal or species that we must recognize.

D: True. Their best argument would be to exploit the necessity of species' existence for the purposes of aesthetics.

However, we have no right to be mean to animals or anybody else as that is the promulgation of misery.

H: I agree. But I suppose we do come into some contracts with animals, an example of which would be our household pets which would be that you, the pet, provide company, and I'll provide food and shelter.

D: Right.

H: But anyway, I guess we have digressed from our subject of abortion which for my part I have no more questions. I would like, though, to ask you about the phrase that we have heard occasionally which is that the end justifies the means. We spoke of this when speaking of revolutionaries.

D: Yes.

H: We stated that the end does not justify the means, but I do not think that I could explain why.

D: You are speaking of the problem where there is some sort of result that someone would like to effect, but the problem is that the only way to the result is through some unethical actions such as the breaking of a contract, or some other disrespectful act which could range right up to the worst possible actions.

H: Yes. I am thinking especially of those politicians, as we discussed before, who have tried to effect a utopia of one sort or another and have resorted to any and all means, no matter how draconian the measures, to meet their utopian goal or dream that they or some ideologue has envisioned.

D: And so, the question is whether the ultimate goal, which is considered ethical, could be attained through unethical means and yet retain a semblance of ethicality to the process and the situation.

H: I feel it can. For example, if a deadly virus were to break out in a specific location and a political leader was advised by his country's medical experts to quarantine the area off so that nobody could get in or out and that this would prevent the outbreak of the deadly virus into the general public, he would be doing an ethical act in that he is trying to prevent the general population of his country from contracting the deadly virus but at the same time he is being tragically disrespectful to the few condemned victims of the virus within the infected area and even more tragically disrespectful to those in the quarantine zone that have not been infected with the virus, although already possibly exposed to it, still not showing signs of contraction and who would like to get out of the quarantine zone. It seems to me that although it is a heart-rending decision, the political leader is making an ethical decision, and his objection, or end, is ethical, that is, trying to save his country from the deadly viral infection; but on the way to the end, he has to be harshly disrespectful (he essentially signs their death warrant sacrificing their lives) to some people (the means) and hence, here at least the end justifies the means. But it would be difficult in my mind at least to be able to distinguish between this example and another example whereby the leader has this objective which he believes is good and he is willing to employ any means to obtain his goal. How do we know when to respect the rights of the individual as opposed to seeking the good for the group or society as a whole?

D: Well, the end, or the objective, cannot reign supreme over the means or the individual. The end justifies the means is in other words the valuing of an objective to the exclusion of the importance of the means which is the value of the individuals involved in obtaining this end. The end justifies the means is the objective and is all to the exclusion of the good for the individual.

H: It seems that at least sometimes the attainment of some ends are justified.

D: As we expatiated before, the individual is the first parameter of the survival of society. If the individuals do not have the ability to follow their self-interests and do not perform to their potential, this takes away from the survival of society as a whole. The second parameter, as we discussed, is the cooperation of the individuals. Cooperation is nothing but contracts between people or between people and society or government.   Within the contracts are the understandings between the parties which are the rights of the people involved. In order to be ethical, cooperative behavior must operate within the contracts to afford the individuals their self-interest. The vehicle by which these contracts and agreements operate is respect. Hence, the end never justifies the means: it is a statement that is not relevant to ethics. The ethical end is that which operates within the contracts of society or within the confines of the rules and laws of cooperation within society.

H: Then, how do you explain my two examples?

D: The first, involving the despot who seeks to place the society over which he rules into his vision of utopia, is unethical no matter if his objective is the most wonderful of all. This is because he will probably have to operate outside the cooperative contracts and understandings that the people of his society have with its government which will probably hold that there must be respect for their individual lives if they do nothing criminal. If the ruler initiates a pogrom, forced labor camps or any of the other horrible grisly things that we have read about throughout history, and even current history at that, he operates outside the contractual understandings of society with government. In the second example, where the ruler makes a hard and fast choice of constructing a quarantine that he envisions will do the greatest good for his people, he probably operates within the understandings of his society because most likely his society has the covenant that one of the purposes of the government is to protect its constituents, and the ruler prescribing the quarantine fits within this understanding even though he has to condemn some individuals to the tragic unfortunate misery of the vile disease.

H: Why do you keep saying "probably"?

D: I say it because we have not delineated what the society's contracts are which would be its rules, regulations, covenants, and laws. It is just probable that those understandings are within society's understandings because these understandings were very basic, and it seems reasonable that in most societies those covenants regarding the respect of their lives by the government would be expected by the constituents. I would hope that you, Haskell, would expect that our government would hold your own life as important, and it would take any action against you only with due cause.

H: Yes. You're right. It is natural to our self-interest to wish it so and to hope that the other societies around the world would be of the same nature and ideal.

D: And at the risk of sounding repetitive, the best way to ensure the government's sincere consideration of the understandings of society and of the sanctity of individuals within society, is by the emplacement of democracy as we know that individuals act with their self-interest first and the transference of this ethic to the government by means of voting helps ensure that government is respectful of its duty to be sincere and cooperative toward one and all.

H: Yes. Let me now ask about how we make ethical judgments in general. It would seem that we should, as we have done in these few problems I have asked about, apply our standard of ethics and see where it leads us.

D: Certainly.

H: In making our judgments, as I asked when we began this whole conversation about how to know if one person should not do this or that, we need to refer to the standard of ethics.

D: Yes, if it is a problem of good and bad in behavior, then our standard of ethics can be applied. When you asked about whether one type of behavior exhibited by the fellow who was withdrawn and did not want to work much and just sat around and listened to music is better compared to the behavior of the industrious fellow, we can make a judgment as to which person is ethically superior in behavior because we can put up our ethical standard and make this judgment. However, you also wondered whether you should follow your father's directions and go to law school or not. This is a decision that would use only the first parameter of ethics because it only involves you, and that is, how well will going to law school serve you in the quandary of your own particular problem of survival, or in other words, living your life? It is a personal question that only you can work out for yourself according to your own wishes, goals, values, likes or dislikes. But when it becomes a social issue, we invoke the second parameter which is based in the survival of the group and manifested by cooperation which is nothing else but mutual understandings and contracts.

H: You just mentioned the concept of "values." That is a word that is often used today in phrases such as "family values, social values, and personal values." What do you suppose is the meaning of this word? I suspect that it has to do with a person's priorities.

D: Yes. That's right. Values are the preferential selections of those things with which people are concerned. One must choose the relative good of everything that comes into his life and this set of preferences and priorities demonstrates a person's values. Thus, a person's family values would be how important the matters of his family are. One's choices in how he structures the family would collectively be called a person's "family values."

H: That's simple and clear enough. Let me ask you another question that is prevalent in contemporary social conversation. It is the matter of a political force of one geographical area, whether of Europe, Asia, or wherever, penetrating a new land and displacing the aboriginal inhabitants of the new land such as the Europeans coming to North America and displacing the native Indians or the British in Australia or any other displacement that has happened throughout history. In earlier times historians generally called it migrations such as the Angles, Saxons, and the Jutes to England where the Kelts were already. First, would you say that these migrations are ethical, or are they unethical as is the popular opinion today especially when the conversation of the American Indian comes up? And secondly, could imperialism be an ethical policy of a country such as Britain began to pursue in the latter half of the nineteenth century? I am making a distinction between migration and imperialism which I will define as foreign rule of a territory without its incorporation into a unified country.

D: All right. I'll accept that distinction. And to answer your question: yes, to both parts; it can be ethical.

H: How is that? Start with the displacement of the American Indian. Was it ethical?

D: We know that ethics is the study of good and bad in behavior and it is based on survival. We also know that in order to further survival cooperation is needed and the vehicle that provides this in our behavior is respect. Furthermore, the essence of cooperation is the contract. We understand that in interacting with someone, we expect the other person to behave in a certain expected fashion. If it does not happen, we decide that cooperation is not being performed and we modify our understandings accordingly. These understandings within the contract are known as rights. If there are no agreements or contracts, there are no rights. The American Indians were of primitive societies with only a few contracts in place. These social contracts were within each tribe with very little cooperation being projected outside this social unit. Hence, there are few, delineated rights in their society. There were no property rights, and hence, no one owned anything except his very personal items if even that. If another group of people begins to assemble and start to effect contracts that further cooperation that help to further ensure survival for themselves and the more primitive people, it is ethical that the more advanced people appear and further the society, and hence, everybody's survival. However, it is not ethical for the more advanced people to act in a deleteriously prejudicial manner toward a weaker less advanced society and subjugate them such that the opportunities to take advantage of the improved society are not available to them. This would obviously be unethical because it is not promoting the enhancement of their survival and would be causing misery instead.

H: Interesting. So the migration of the English, the French, the Irish, and so on to the New World displacing the Indians was ethical because the new society that they were manufacturing was more advanced and more capable of furthering the survival of mankind. And so we can conclude that it is good that they migrated and began to establish a more advanced society. But in order to make the migration ethical, the migrants must offer to assimilate the more primitive society and give them the more advanced opportunities inherent in the more cooperative society.

D: Correct. As long as there are advancements and opportunities for the general survival of society, it is ethical.

H: What about imperialism? I suppose we could say that imperialism is ethical if the new governing society brings with it advancements for the denizens of the territory.

D: Yes, but rarely do governments of countries, when operating extraterritorially, exhibit such benign, ethical, altruistic, magnanimous characteristics. The only way imperialism can work is if the new government, as soon as possible, sets up a democratic republic to ensure that the general interests of society are being promoted.

H: Yes. I agree. How about a forceful invasion? Can it be ethical? Obviously, Hitler's invasions and others like it were not, but there might be some, possibly. For example, was Knute's invasion of England from Denmark in 865, ethical? Or how about William's invasion of England in 1066, or maybe Rome's conquest of Gaul and the Mediterranean area? And for that matter, since our forebears had some run-in with the Indians, perhaps this problem is not yet solved.

D: We should look at the problem categorically. First is that, yes, the settlers of America did have battles with the Indians, but that does not make the migration and proliferation of a more extensively cooperative society unethical.

Unfortunately, they occurred. And it was furthermore unfortunate that the Indian tribes each for the most part could not recognize that the European settlers had much to offer in the advancement of life. The migration basically brought a developing cooperation which held within it the furthering of life to another continent, and hence overall, it was good and therefore ethical. On the other hand, any war for the sake of rapine or the subjugation of other people is categorically unethical: the objective is unethical and there will necessarily be disrespect of the individuals of the other society, and hence, in such a case we would have evil. However, there may be a war where a group of people are being pushed into other territories or looking to move because of some reason linked to their survival such as the need for farmland or resources, and they would like to settle in another place but are being met with resistance. Both sides feel uncomfortable with each other. Both sides have ethical concerns and objectives, and it would be impossible to say if there is a bad party to the resulting actions. If the objective is essential in terms of that society's survival, and thusly, ethical, and all means except violence are eliminated, then the last resort is war. It is a sometime occurrence that is incumbent to living on this earth due to one's own predicament and to the factors of free will and risk as we discussed previously. Hence, sometimes war is justified and ethical to pursue such as the American Civil War. However, a war where the invaders come for subjugation and rapine is obviously horribly anti-ethical as it does not exhibit the appropriate dispensation of respect.

H: I see. We must again apply our standard of ethics to even problems of war to find the understandings of its ethicality. And when we apply our standard to problems of the study of the good and bad in behavior, do we know for sure that we are right? Are we right to say that we know the good or the right or the just more than the next man when we make a conclusion about a problem in good and bad, or that is, in ethics? I think that we discussed this briefly, but I would like to go over it again.

D: Yes, we did. As in the pursuit of any knowledge, we try to consider it completely, and over time the probability that our understanding is correct will increase and we will become more confident of our conclusions. We put forward our standard of ethics for examination, and if there is not a better system and our understanding of its essence holds up under prolonged examination, then the probability of its cogency and correctness will increase and approach surety. What we have done in these sessions is put forward an understanding of the essence of ethics. We described its basis from which all ethical behavior is derived. We know that all good behavior is based on survival, that individual survival is perpetuated by self-interest, that social survival is effected by cooperation, that cooperation consists of contracts and within contracts there are rights and wrongs and the do's and the don'ts that are ascribed to the contracts of cooperation by the participants. A most famous delineation of rights and wrongs is the New and Old Testaments of the Bible which describes rules not only for how we should live in this world but also it notes what should be done if we want to live after living in this world which we might conclude is a subsequent and greater survival. Secondary to the laws of the Bible (or other documents depending on one's faith) would be the diurnal laws of the society in which we live and are put down by Congress, signed by the President (usually), and committed to the

Federal Register. Thirdly, added to that would be the contracts of business followed by personal understandings between ourselves and the folks we meet in our daily lives. And the adherence to the contracts and understandings is enabled by the vehicle of respect.

H: Yes, I understand. But let's go back to our discussion of war and conflict. There is a derivative problem that comes up when we speak of war or some sort of physical discord. I am wondering, is there an ethical basis by which a person can know whether to involve himself in an antagonism that is already being waged?

D: I don't follow you.

H: Suppose there is a regional conflict, or a war if you will, that does not involve our society, but we think that one side has the moral high ground: is it ethically permissible to enter this conflict and choose a side even though we have no self-interest involved in this struggle?

D: Yes, I understand your question.

H: My problem, in addition to the issue of intervention in a regional conflict, pertains to any situation where someone or some society has no apparent interest in a dispute between two or more other parties. It is the question of whether intervention in another's problem, dispute, conflict, or war is ethically permissible when we have no apparent self-interest or survival motive. It seems to me that there needs to be this basis of self-interest for anything to be ethical. So if there is a conflict and we have no self-interest in it, then there can be no ethical incentive or basis by which intervention can be effected. And yet, I feel that although there appears to be no ethical basis for intervention, I am uneasy about the possible conclusion that this thought leads me.

D: You mean that if there is no ethical basis to intervene in a conflict then one should not. And you feel that this conclusion is an uncomfortable one.

H: Yes, because I feel that there are times when one should intervene, or I should say, I know there are times or circumstances when I would want to intervene, even though it appears through our discussions that perhaps we would have no ethical basis. As an illustration, let's say that I am walking down the street and I come upon a man brutally beating or violating a woman and she calls out for help. I do not know them and am not involved with them in any way and I believe there is no in-place contracts between us although there might be one in place between the two of them and between them and society, that is, the government. Therefore, I believe, as I understand the nature of ethics, to have no ethical basis by which I should take it upon myself to intervene and prevent the conflict between this man and woman and stop his assault on her. Yet, I know that my feelings are otherwise. I know that I would like to - nay, even should - intervene to save her from further misery. But nevertheless, it seems that it is the ethical province of the society's government to intervene and straighten this brutal situation out.

D: Your feelings are admirable, and therein my response of approbation lies the answer to the problem.

H: How so?

D: My innate spontaneous response was to applaud your action, or thought that is, as this is hypothetical. Even though we recognize that there is no apparent contractual relationship between you and the man and woman, you lend your strength to the situation to alleviate the impartation of misery that is being conveyed from the man to the woman. And you do so because, although you lack the apparent ethical basis, you proceed out of conscience and your sense of aesthetics to invoke that which should be in this world. As you will recall from our discussions on the nature of aesthetics, aesthetics itself is also steeped in survival and that which is the ultimate in evolution, and it is necessary that we can recognize the pinnacle in evolution.

H: But still, what is the basic ethical foundation by which I would rationalize my grounds for intervention in a situation that I perceive as unjust and terrible because we previously established that without a contractual agreement, there are no rights? All rights emanate from agreements, and I perceive that I have no contract in place when I walk past this violent situation where an injustice is occurring.

D: You may intervene upon your own choosing and assessment of the situation because you may invoke an immediate blanket contract to cover situations of general societal injustice. Along the same lines whence the concept of a citizen's arrest derives, the intervention into an obvious societal injustice may occur by an ordinary citizen even if he is not a functionary of society with the power of keeping the peace. This concept of intervention comes from the general contract in society that members will cooperate together to live in peace. And hence, it is incumbent upon each member to show the very basic origins of respect for this cooperation which entails a non-aggressive behavior that avoids the violation of the person. And hence, the individual citizen has the obligation to respect the others around him, and in order to promote the general well-being of society, the conceptual social contract of mutual assistance to keep the peace evolves as exhibited by the idea of the citizen's arrest.

H: So I could invoke this nebulous contract that the denizens of society have with each other that indicates that there is a voluntary right by which each citizen has an incumbency to keep the peace, and should he wish to invoke this societal contractual obligation to intervene in a situation to prevent or quell a simple injustice, he may do so.

D: Correct.   And I assume that you used the phrase "simple injustice" because obviously if it is an extensive, complicated injustice it would quickly be out of the abilities of the single individual to efficiently rectify the unjust situation and become the province of an organization set up to handle such problems such as a private or public police force and judicial system.

H: Yes, but let me ask, is it obligatory in a society to have this concept of the citizen's arrest or the right to intervene in a simple societal injustice? Could the person happening upon the injustice pass it by without intervention and still be within his rights, that is, and still be considered ethical?

D: To answer the first question, society can state for all to know that there shall be no contract within the society that shall call for a citizen's arrest or for individual intervention within an obvious situation of injustice, and there would be no right as declared. However, one's conscience may not be satisfied with this for the reasons that we just a little bit ago touched upon when we spoke of our general will to reduce misery and this feeling and thought to be of the aesthetic.

H: I see.

D: And to address the second question of whether can you choose not to participate in negating the injustice, the answer is simply that one can because the contract in place does not delineate that the citizen must participate. He assesses the situation and decides what are the consequences to him if he enters the fray, whether he can afford the energy, and how much his conscience will weigh in the matter. But there is no overall obligation to join in.

H: Yes, I see. What about some of the other situations I mentioned such as when countries are involved? Can one country ethically join one side or another especially when there is no organizational documentation that announces a pact or alliance between two or more nations whereby each will come to the aid of the other should an outside aggression occur? It seems to me we will not find the concept of a citizen's arrest helpful to us when the fray becomes a large complicated one that involves more than the lone individual.

D: Yes. If there were no contract of any kind in place, then there would be no obligatory rights that could be invoked by one of the countries to draw a third country into the conflict.

H: Therefore, if there were no obligatory involvement in which to intervene, it would seem to me that there would be no ethical platform by which non-treaty situational intervention would be possible.

D: But there can be a justification for intervention even though there may be no delineating agreement that would establish the ethical basis by which rights are defined and intervention expected and obligatory.

H: How so?

D: Even though there is no agreement in place, intervention can be ethically understandable if the third country decides truly that the amount of injustice and misery happening in the conflict is beyond conscience's limit of tolerance and the consequences and extent of misery that would be self-inflicted upon one's country would not be extensive.

H: The only deciding factor is one's own conscience, and its subjective weighing of its conscience and its realization of the other country's misery versus the potential for self-inflicted misery. I find this a very nebulous factor when we tie it to that which is ethical. Your statement seems to equate one's own conscience to what is right and wrong and what is ethical: it would depend on the extent that a country's leader has a conscience and how the injustices of the conflict weigh upon the mind.

D: Well, as everybody knows, the political process is not a perfect one, and if there is to be a government and a leader of a government, then hopefully the leader of that government will mirror the values of the majority of the political constituents; and a country's decision to participate in a conflict is the same decision-making process as an individual's. And in our situation where a country is to decide whether to enter a conflict, the decision to join an international fray takes on the same process as if it were an individual deciding whether to enter into a conflict between two others outside of his society (and hence, not even the citizen's arrest rationalization could be invoked).

H: So you are saying that conscience is our only deciding factor where no ties or relationship of any kind has been established?   But if so, as I asked just a bit ago, isn't conscience too nebulous to use to know if some action is ethical?

D: No. Conscience is the means by which misery is measured and the dispensation of respect toward others is accorded. When we view a situation where respect is not in accordance with the subject's production and misery is being dispensed by some agent or another, our conscience evaluates this process and the more there is an imbalance, the more the pangs of conscience strike us.

H: But still there is no cogent ethical basis by which we must intervene in a conflict based on the flimsy excuse that it upsets our conscience.

D: I disagree. Conscience is important, and because of its capacity to weigh the amount of disrespect being handed out and its capacity to recognize the dispensation of misery, conscience is part of the mechanism of ethical decision-making. If we see widespread misery being handed out, conscience gives us the urge to do something about it. Our conscience's capacity to recognize misery and any incongruous proportionate dispensation of respect allows us to make decisions that we can deem ethical. And if conscience sees too much disrespect and misery, a feeling of obligation will descend upon us out of our individual or national conscience to do something to rectify the situation.

H: Hence, there are two ways by which one can interject oneself into a situation of conflict: first is by adherence to delineated rights embedded in some sort of an agreement for which one is a party, and the other way is by conscience.

D: Yes.

H: You stated that man's conscience is that which determines the appropriate amount of respect due to those within our ken. Is it that and only that?

D: Yes. Every time you make a decision which involves the conscience it is measuring the respect involved in the situation and seeing if the dispensation of the respect stacks up to the appropriate amount that the conscience dictates that there should be.

H: I am not sure I follow. How about an example?

D: Sure. Let's take our case of the guy walking down the street and coming upon the man violating the woman. Irregardless of any contracts that may or may not be in place indicating whether or not you have any obligation to involve yourself, you will assess the situation and your conscience will tell you whether there is a situation that needs correcting based on the amounts of respect being given and received in the situation. In this case, your conscience easily decides that the woman is not receiving the respect due to her as a member of society and in fact it is such a gross disparity that your conscience brings you to the possible conclusion that you should get involved to rectify the situation. In the second case where a country decides whether to intervene in a regional conflict somewhere even though it has no explicit obligation and it is not a matter of self-defense, the country will weigh the situation in terms of whether there has been, is, and will be atrocities or pogroms against a populous so great that the country's collective conscience dictates involvement to stop or preempt the atrocities, and these atrocities are nothing else but the obvious lack of respect for human life by an aggressor.

H: I see. Let's take a more difficult example. What about the shooting or hunting of an animal? Why do some people hunt and kill, and others think it very wrong to do so? Can this be explained in terms of respect and the conscience? As there are no rights that can be afforded the animals because there are no agreements in place, the obvious conclusion would be that there is no reason not to be able to hunt or kill them.

D: The differences, in the way we assess the situation for the conscience, provide us the difference in whether one person prefers hunting while another does not. One person will consider hunting (which, by the way, may be biologically induced) as a primitive game and the meat and skin as the reward of the game's conclusion which at one time in the not-too-distant past could have been an actual way of life and an absolute necessity for one and one's family. Another person not having that particular sentiment would have his conscience assessing the situation as hunting not attributing the proper amount of respect to the animal concluding that it is a higher form of life, and therefore should be accorded more respect than a lower form, such as an insect, and not be wantonly hunted and killed only to satisfy some small primitive urge when no great real need to hunt exists, and the misery being dealt to this higher life form, which is a common denizen of the earth, would be much greater than the satisfaction of the urge.

H: It appears that we cannot universally conclude that hunting just for the sport of it is ethically wrong because there are no particular rights that are delineated or understood anywhere, therefore, there can be no quantification of respect due to the animal, and, of course, the hunter is not hit with any pangs of conscience because he is not cognizant of any disparity of dispensation in the accordance of respect because he places his own will to enjoy the sport above any respect due the animal or above the misery being dispensed by his action. We know that hunters as a whole do not like to inflict extended misery on their kills. As a category, they seek to end the life of their prey as efficiently as possible and consume the meat which exhibits their respect for the game.

D: Correct.

H: Well, I think I have a more difficult problem for whether the conscience is our instrument of respect. I heard on a radio news program the other day about witnesses watching in a Near East city market area a camel being skinned alive while the camel, of course, was screaming out in obvious pain of the worst sort while the men were laughing about it. It is obvious that they gave the camel no further respect, it being probably old and no longer could be used for transport and its only value was for its skin and for that, they just stripped it off the animal. I thought as I heard the report indicate that the men had no conscience, and at the same time, I was outraged that the men did not even bother with a bullet in the head of the camel to alleviate its impending pain.

D: Right. You were affected by the story because your conscience told you that the camel deserved at least the respect of it not having to suffer such pain. And you were outraged because if we remember our definition of evil which is the lack of respect toward others along with an unethical objective, you might have sensed the smell of a little bit of evil here.

H: Yes, I did. Obviously, it does not take much of a conscience to see that the camel is not being afforded the minimum respect of killing it so it does not have to endure the awful pain, but in addition, I suspect from the fact that the men were laughing that there may have been the unethical objective of causing the animal intentionally the awful pain.

D: You may be right. Now let me conclude my comments of conscience by saying that the conscience's purpose is to dispense with the appropriate amount of respect to others so that we may cooperate within society for the purpose of production which ensures our survival and adds to our quality of living.

Chapter 5

The Nature of That Which Is Better

H:Yes, I see. You said something a little bit ago as we started on the subject of the conscience that I found interesting. You not only talked about the emergence of the conscience as a vehicle in helping us make behavioral decisions but also about the inclusion of the sense of aesthetics being important and that it also was steeped in survival. I did not quite understand what you had in mind. What is the connection between the aesthetic sense, and our conscience, misery, and ethics?

D: I mentioned aesthetics because if we recall its essence, that which is the pinnacle (the positive extreme) of that which has evolved, and if we have a sharp conscience sensitive to that which is right and wrong though its power to determine that which is due respect and that this is important to man's being, then to have an excellent conscience is to be of the aesthetic and the more something is aesthetic, the better it is. Adding in our sense of aesthetics enables us to decide as we can by our conscience to understand discrepancies in the levels of respect to be imparted to those with whom we come into contact, which enables us to construct our ethical understanding which is the judgment of good and bad in behavior which not only enables us to make decisions that on the whole lead us away from the eruption and dispensation of misery, but also allows us to decide that which is of value in this world and what is better and best in our judgments, critiques, and assessments of not only behavior but for things of life in general as well.

H: What on earth do you mean?

D: Do you remember your own example of the sloth and the diligent fellow and whether we can judge and know which fellow is doing good and whether we can say that the sloth-like fellow is not as good as the other?

H: Yes.

D: And then we launched ourselves into this subject of ethics which is the judgment of good and bad in behavior.

H: Yes.

D: We determined that the diligent fellow is more in line with the ethical life; it is not that we determined that the sloth fellow is unethical, but that he was not so much in keeping with the ideal ethical way and cannot be considered to possess much ethics. And the fellow who is not as industrious as the next is not as ethical as the industrious fellow because the ethical is based on respect and that one accords respect to those that cooperatively produce in their lives. But in addition, when we mix in our aesthetic sense, we know that the more one produces, the more one establishes a platform by which we further stabilize our lives, and further ensure our survival, reduce misery, and further the goodness of our lives; furthermore, the more one produces, the more one will be considered of the good (i.e. better) because our aesthetic sense tells us that it is so; as this producer is more of a positive extreme: he is more cooperative, he is more productive, he is securing his survival for himself and for those to whom he is responsible. He is, according to aesthetics, better because he is more of the positive extreme, more adaptative, and the more likely to survive.

H: Let's review this a bit. Are you saying by our aesthetic sense we may not only know what is ethical and not ethical but also know what is more ethical than another thing?

D: Yes.

H: So, of course, the fellow who was not as productive, watched a lot of television, did not apply himself that much, did not care for those around him as much as another, and was more interested in his own personal simple pleasures is known as not necessarily unethical, but because of our sense of aesthetics, we know that he is not as ethical and wonderful as the very productive, respectful fellow.

D: Yes.

H: Let me point out that according to this line of thought the person who has the least time for his own pleasure is the one who is the most ethical and aesthetic person. When may we have personal pleasure and still be ethical?

D: Well, the ethical person may resort to personal pleasure as his obligations to his various contracts and agreements are fulfilled. As the contracts, agreements, and understandings that envelop his life become more complicated and involved, the less he can spend on his own time for personal pleasure.

H: So, if a person marries and has children, right there with that contract in place the obligations toward one's wife and children take up his time considerably as they make immediate demands of his time. He must work to get money to support his family obligations, he must work around the house on the weekends to get his place running smoothly and the list goes on. Yes, I can see that just by that marriage contract his time would diminish for personal pleasure when compared to a bachelor.

D: Yes. He must fulfill his obligations in order to take the occasional time out for personal pleasure. In addition, the more he provides (production) for his family, the more he becomes of the aesthetical because the more he provides, the better it is for his family and for those that have entered into agreements with him.

H: I see. So in conclusion, ethics tells us what is the good and bad in our behavior and aesthetics tells us what is better or best in not only ethics but in art, sports, or whatever.

D: Correct. Our aesthetic sense is the vehicle by which we may know whether one thing is better than another as aesthetics tells us what is the positive extreme or that which is most adaptative. As something lends itself to being adaptative, the more one can provide for overall survival and the more one is better and hence, more aesthetic.

H: You seem to equate production to be the key by which ethics and aesthetics are considered and by which all things are known to be better than another thing. You seem to be saying that the more one produces, the more one is ethical and the more one is aesthetic.

D: It cannot be quantified quite like that because we must remember that ethics is not production itself, but it is related to production through respect. Earlier we established that ethics is that which is the good in behavior and this good is provided by respect which is the vehicle by which we consider others which facilitates cooperation in order to produce goods and services that are necessary to ensure and further our survival. Hence, I would prefer to state that the more one is respectful, the more one is ethical as we noted at the beginning of our discussion. To relate this to aesthetics, we should note that respect, consideration, cooperation, and production are all things that would be considered aesthetic when a high degree of it is present. When we see a very respectful person who is aesthetic and we see consideration of others and excellent cooperation among people who are trying to produce something that is beneficial for society to survival, we are pleased as it appeals to our aesthetic sense. Aesthetics is the positive extreme, and when we see a greater degree of that which is beneficial in survival, we sense the aesthetic as we discussed in our previous conversation. And so, when considering ethics and those components of ethics such as respect as they become more prevalent, salient, bountiful, or greater in degree, we will notice that because of its beneficial aspects, these components of ethics and ethical behavior in its entirety become more aesthetic.

H: I see. Detmar, I would like to thank you for your time again. It has been a very interesting discussion and I look forward to the next time.

D: I also will look forward to it.

H: Again, thanks.

D: Come back anytime.

H: I will. Good-bye for now.

www.ingramcontent.com/pod-product-compliance
Lightning Source LLC
Chambersburg PA
CBHW051318120626
46547CB00015B/2292